ALPHA KINGS

The Roadmap For Every Young Man To Unlock Their Full Potential

By Nick Adams

Foreword by President Donald J. Trump

Stay strong,
King!

NICK

Table of Contents

The Alpha Male Creed

I am an alpha male.

I embrace my natural masculinity without apology.

I radiate confidence and charisma, inspiring others to embrace their own strength and strive for excellence.

I transform setbacks into stepping stones.

I uphold the timeless traditional values of faith, family, honor, and integrity.

I am committed to preserving liberty and protecting the Constitution.

In the face of adversity, I remain unshakeable.

I am fueled by my love of country and my foundation is built on faith in God.

I am an alpha male.

FOREWORD

By President Donald J. Trump

When my good friend Nick Adams asked me to write a foreword for his important new book on alpha males, I didn't have to think twice about it. For the last several years, I have admired Nick's tenacity, guts, and patriotism.

It's one thing to be born and raised in the United States and to appreciate all that this country offers. But when somebody comes from another land and wants nothing more than to be an American, to uphold American values and patriotic spirit, it's something that I truly appreciate. That's Nick Adams.

Nick has become one of my favorite authors and also one of my favorite public speakers. His intelligence, courage, and sense of humor make him a force to be reckoned with as the stakes become even higher in defending this country's constitution against ever-increasing negative forces, both from within and on the outside.

I trust and admire Nick so much that I have asked him to become, as of the writing of this book, a surrogate for my upcoming presidential campaign. The concept of this new book, helping men reclaim their Alpha status, is an important one. Nick is leading the movement towards helping men, young and old alike, appreciate and reclaim what made this country great in the first place.

Like me, I know that Nick appreciates the power of humor, when it comes to making a point, but there are also very serious things contained in this book. Reminding young men of the importance of faith in God, hard work, sports, ambition, discipline, confidence, manners, and love of country is a very important task and Nick embraces that challenge with gusto, knowledge, and heart.

When you put yourself out there in the public eye as he does, you know you are going to get many attacks upon everything, from your character to your family. But when you believe in something as strongly as Nick does, it doesn't matter. He's so committed to fighting for the qualities that make alpha males so special that nothing will stand in his way. I don't think you'll find too many politicians that Nick will call an alpha, and I don't take that lightly.

I know you will enjoy Nick's many stories, tips, and advice when it comes to embracing an alpha male identity. He's a very good writer, he's a very strong thinker and he is someone who knows how to reach his audience effectively, efficiently, and successfully. He knows that to educate, you have to entertain.

He's the kind of person I would always look to hire at my many businesses because his work ethic equals his moral responsibility and faith in God. In my opinion, that's what we need more of these days and Nick, I just want to wish you all the best with this book.

Again, it's a privilege to add my words to this foreword and I look forward to continuing watching your career grow and thrive in the name of true American values.

Great work, Nick. You're a true patriot.

Introduction

I can't count the number of times I have been discouraged from writing this book.

In fact, even Simon & Schuster, the publishing powerhouse who distributed my last seven books, backed away.

Three copy editors turned down the work.

Even the researcher I contracted and paid to assist with this book got cold feet and tried to undermine it from within. Turns out he is one the greatest beta males I have ever come across.

This is the book that they tried to kill.

The book the Left doesn't want you to read.

The one that will explode the heads of liberal feminist women and effeminate men.

They are afraid of this book. They are afraid of me.

You see, over the course of the last two years, I have found myself leading a massive and rapidly developing movement of young men aged between 15-35. These young men love America, love sports, have traditionally male interests and activities, and are sick of being told that their masculinity is toxic and that their generation will and should be led by women.

Thank you to the greatest President of my lifetime, and the most alpha world leader since Winston Churchill, the forty-fifth and forty-seventh President of the United States, for writing the foreword. You remain an inspiration to people everywhere, particularly young men. No one can absorb the attacks and the pressure that you have daily and still prevail. You are a study in peak alpha masculinity for the ages.

The modern woke feminists and the dishonest media that prop up their sexist ideology are terrified because I'm organizing thousands of alpha males in a way that hasn't been done since Dwight Eisenhower assembled the troops to storm the beaches of Normandy in 1944. This chills their bones and freezes their sweat because they know that organizing the alpha male demographic is more impactful than any other – because alphas get things done.

This is why I have become one of the most attacked men in America. I am known by all and loved by many, but the hate directed at me is red-hot.

I never sought this position. It just happened this way.

I am a straight Christian male, and proud of it. I love women. I admire the female form. When I see a good-looking woman, I make no apologies for checking her out. I can't help it; it's how God made me. I am a man, and I'm not ashamed of it. No matter how much woke feminists and betas want to neuter me, they can't and won't.

I'm also a man that generally prefers the company of other men. I know many women might not like to hear that, and I don't say it to offend. It's just the truth. I've always been what they call a 'man's man.' Much of it probably has to do with how and where I grew up. I went to an all-boys school from K-12. Growing up in one of the most multicultural cities in the world, Sydney, Australia, my friends came from many varied backgrounds. In all those cultures, to this day, even when married and present at a social function, the men congregate with the men, and the women congregate with the women. When there is a school reunion, no one brings their spouse or 'significant other.' I know this to be true in Germany and Greece as well.

I know America is different, but more on that later. Back to me for the time being.

I enjoy the finer things in life. I like ice-cold domestic beer, good wine, the odd shot of ouzo, and an occasional Basil Hayden bourbon. As anyone who follows me on social media also knows, I enjoy watching sports at Hooters over some Daytona-style wings and a cold domestic draft!

And so, it just happened that I became Twitter's Top Alpha, and a very prominent voice for Generation Z and Millennial men. Young men all over the country were drawn to my unapologetic and strident masculine messaging, humor, guidance, and encouragement.

Even the conservative movement, which I am a creature of, has been wholly swallowed up – creating an entire industry of female outreach, buttressed by all-women conferences. That's great; I've spoken at those regularly.

But what about men? Why are there no conferences – either on the liberal or conservative sides – for men?

Somebody needed to do it, and Nick Adams (Alpha Male) stepped up to fill the void.

I've built this movement myself. My father always taught me: *If nobody will help you, do it alone.* So that's what we have done, and what we will continue to do.

I'm the proudest American you will ever meet. The day I became a citizen was the greatest day of my life.

I've had the good fortune of being able to spend a lot of time around the world, and it gives me a perspective on many things that others born in this country might not have.

So let me start with this bombshell. In the United States of America, women have defined what a man is. This makes America unique in the world.

This isn't the case anywhere else that I know.

Of course, in the old world cultures – and there are many – Greeks, Italians, Indians, Egyptians, Spanish, French, Portuguese and Lebanese – as you might expect, men define what men are.

But this is also the case in our country's most steadfast ally, another very young country – my former homeland – Australia. When it comes to male influence in the national culture, Australia ranks highly. On a few occasions over the years, I have had young American military personnel comment to me – *"I was shocked how much it is still a man's world down there."*

So, let's not pussyfoot around and get straight to it:

This is the best country in the world for anyone to live in, but it is the hardest one to be a man in. Conversely, it is the easiest nation to be a woman in. That's my opinion, but from the messages I receive every day from my followers, it's one held by many.

Now I must tell you, like anyone who grows up in certain circumstances, you always assume that what you have is the status quo. I'm ashamed to say it, but it took me many years to realize that America is a *"woman's world."*

Now that is not all bad. Please make no mistake. I love women. The truth is Americans give, on average, three times more to charity than Europeans, for example, and while there are a few reasons for this, I think an often overlooked one is that the United States is a female-led culture. Women care a lot more and want to give more; it's in their nature. That's a very good thing.

Similarly, the incomparably strong mentoring tradition in America is probably also owed in part to the strength of females in the culture. It is common for older men to take on the position that nobody helped them, they did it themselves, they worked it out - so they don't need to help anybody. Women think differently.

Even the strength and perseverance of the American dream throughout the American experience, I think, can be partly apportioned to women. Men tend to have less patience and a more pragmatic approach to life and career.

And most of all – it is true that women make a kinder, nicer society, and the USA is filled with the kindest and nicest people I have ever encountered.

Nothing in this book is radical. It might be old-fashioned, but so what? Just because we live in 2023 doesn't mean that we automatically know everything better. In the pages to follow, you will find a lot about male self-improvement.

My greatest goal is to give men their confidence back. I want men to be lions, not pussycats.

I want them to be in control of their life, their family, and their finances. I want them to be the best version of themselves that they can be. I want them to be leaders. I want them to take charge. I don't want them to take crap from their children, their wives, their colleagues – no one. I want them to be kings. Kings of their own world, masters of their own domain – I want them to create their own fiefdom.

If that happens, that is not only good for those men – it is great for all women, and it is great for the country.

More on that later.

Make sure the Fortnite controller is far away, the domestic beer is ice cold, the manspread is wide, and the seat is reclined as far back as possible, and enjoy this book – the one that all the people that hate you don't want you to read!

Stay strong, kings!

Nick Adams

January 2024

Tampa, Florida

Nick's Commandments For Alpha Males

In writing this book, my intention is to lay out a roadmap for every young man to unlock their full potential and protect themselves.

With this as my goal, I created *"Nick's Commandments For Alpha Males"* – a list of declarative statements that summarize my core values canvassed within these pages. They are based on personal experience, the experience of friends, the advice I have received from male and female mentors over the years, and overall research.

I believe men will be healthier, happier, stronger, more protected, and better placed in this world, in both their personal and professional lives, if they were to see their way clear to take on many of these perspectives. I am gravely concerned for the mental health of men.

Again, this is a book for men, written by a man, with the purpose of advancing men. For many, thinking of writing such a book is a thought crime. But to put pen to paper? Let's just say that, well, even the Left might reconsider their position on the death penalty for this one case...

On social media, blue-haired feminists and noodle-armed beta soy boys regularly demand I apologize.

For what?

I've inspired an international movement to restore men to their rightful place at the forefront of society.

I'll never apologize for doing that. That's never going to happen.

They, and the electric vehicles they rode in on, can get bent.

America is going out of business, and we need to do something about it.

If we start teaching our boys to be men before the world teaches them to be women, we may have a fighting chance.

No great civilization has ever survived without strong men, and at age 247, with all available evidence, things don't look too promising for us either right now.

So, if some or many, or maybe even all of *'Nick's 45 Commandments'* cause offense, that's too bad. I'm not anti-female; I'm just pro-male.

You don't have to like the rules, but you should abide by them.

I'm direct, unblinking, and have the courage of my convictions.

Few people talk about what I am writing about in private company, and even fewer publish a book on the subjects for the world to read. But there is no time for injured feelings. We are on the brink. No civilization has ever survived without strong men. *'Nick's Commandments For Alpha Males'* seeks to reinvigorate men for this modern era.

Our schools are failing us. They're raising betas. The difference between how they want men to be and how we need men to be, is night and day.

Our young men today are basically told they should try to behave more like women. The feminizing of men, the feminizing of our culture, the feminizing of family, marriage, and faith cannot go on if we are to remain the greatest nation in the world and save Western civilization. If you want the Chinese or radical Islamists running the world, keep it up.

Not to be braggadocious, but I am unique.

In reading these rules, you will note that some of them are a significant departure from the conventional advice of prominent influencers in the male space.

This is owed to me being a unique man – both in cultural and racial background and experience.

Some of these rules, and the ideas that surround them, I have never heard discussed by anybody in the world publicly.

Read them, dwell on them, accept them, and implement them. Here we go!

Commandments:

- *Success is a low-maintenance woman, not just a hot one.*
- *Balls and brilliance will get you further than your body.*
- *An alpha male is never dominated by anything or anyone. He does the dominating. Alpha males don't go with the flow. They ARE the flow.*
- *The female form will consume you if you do not assert yourself.*
- *Get a prenup, or don't get married at all.*
- *The denial of sex by the male is the most alpha act.*
- *Don't tell a woman everything. Some things in life should only be shared with your father, your brother, your son, and your butcher.*
- *An alpha male doesn't abandon his family.*
- *Alpha males don't take unnecessary risks with their lives.*
- *If you want to make everyone happy, don't be an alpha male. Sell ice cream.*
- *Never apologize.*
- *Competition is good, but being super competitive in everything you do is a childlike quality. Real alphas are relaxed and confident.*
- *The most successful alpha males are not ostentatious.*
- *In a relationship, put down your foot early.*
- *Treat your children like adults, from the age of five.*
- *Consider marrying women from cultures that respect and honor men.*
- *Put your purpose in God and country above all else.*
- *Display emotional control, and never show vulnerability or weakness, and always double down.*
- *Alpha males just say NO to the snip.*
- *Body language is important, as it reflects your mind and spirit.*
- *Always keep betas close because they make the best followers, but don't make the mistake of promoting them to a leadership role because it will come back to bite you.*
- *Alpha males are servant leaders; they don't just fight for themselves - they fight for their tribe.*

- *Border on overconfidence; ego is your friend.*
- *Teach your boys to be men before the world teaches them to be women.*
- *Alphas don't need to take victory laps or spike the ball. Just remain cool, confident and steadfast. Act like you've been there before.*
- *You earn respect, not by blending in, but by standing out. Not by going to TGI Fridays, but by going to Hooters.*
- *Dress more "daddy," less dad.*
- *The value of one's word is bigger than the value of a contract. Your word is your bond.*
- *Be aroused by women that work hard for you and your children and are loyal to a fault — not for the ones with the best makeup and nails and biggest Instagram account.*
- *In a woman, an alpha male needs an asset, not a liability; a partner, not a passenger.*
- *An alpha male refuses to be disrespected, and will let his displeasure be known.*
- *You're the catch, not her.*
- *A man who cares more about his Jordans than his bank account cannot be an alpha.*
- *An alpha male is always the boss. His word is final and should not be questioned.*

Chapter 1
It's All in the Definitions

Standing up for men is something I have been doing for a while.

In October 2013, almost three years before I immigrated to the United States, I sat down with Mrs. Ginni Thomas. For those who do not know, Mrs. Thomas is the wife of legendary Supreme Court Justice Clarence Thomas, who I believe to be one of the greatest Americans to have ever lived.

In a wide-ranging interview about my new book at that time, we somehow made our way to the issue of men's rights.

I told her, "All aspects of male culture have been called into question. Whether it's gathering around on a Sunday afternoon to watch football with a few friends, whether it is going to the range and shooting some guns, whether it is just being a male has now been really been made suspect – and that is a very dangerous thing. We see it coming from all levels of society."

Not long after it was published, I received an email from a producer of Fox & Friends asking me to come on the Show to discuss these comments. I was heading back home to Australia, so the timing didn't work, but I was told to let them know the next time I was back, and they would gladly have me on.

I returned a couple of months later, and on January 16, 2014, I sat down with Elisabeth Hasselbeck, Steve Doocy, and Clayton Morris for an interview on the curvy couch that would end up going viral.

During this interview, I explained that most guys in America are getting squashed under the thumb of Big Feminism and that all that modern feminism had achieved was *'angry women and feminine men.'* I also observed that these difficult circumstances that men had to operate in made them *'sweat more than Paris Hilton doing a crossword'* when it came to decision making, and concluded that *'wimps and wusses deliver mediocrity and real men win.'*

Well, as you might imagine, every feminist and her lesbian sister came after me. That was my first encounter with the handbag hit squad and militant lavender lobby (they had a few less letters back then!)

I'll take the heat; it doesn't bother me. When you had a father as tough as mine, everything else pales in comparison.

I just don't want men to be taken advantage of. Since that interview almost a decade ago, things have become significantly worse for us.

The culture and society in the United States is gravely ill. There is no beta tapdancing that can finesse that reality. As a once-legal immigrant, now-naturalized American citizen, I can't tell you how much this hurts me. Even with all its problems, the US remains the greatest country in the history of the world.

It's still the place that affords the most freedom and opportunity to the maximum number of people. There is still nowhere I would rather wake up. In the last twelve months, when I have traveled to Australia, the Middle East, and Europe, as soon as I land back in the States, I feel like kissing the ground.

But the United States is clearly not what it once was – nor is the culture healthy as it once was. At 38 years old at the time of writing, visiting regularly from the age of 24, and immigrating at 31, I obviously never got to see the country or experience the culture at its zenith.

I wish for a return to that version of America, where the traditional family unit was strong, fatherlessness was rare, there was no dispute that there were only two genders, drag queens were not reading to children in public libraries, and where men were manly, and women were, well, feminine. A place where a man like me is *celebrated* for his success and masculinity, not persecuted for it.

Don't get me wrong. This war on men and the feminization of the culture is happening everywhere. No country or culture is totally immune. It's just a whole lot worse in America. Once more, even around gender relations, America is exceptional as it always is. Except this is one form of exceptionalism that it could do without...

At the crux of everything are two definitions.

These definitions came from women and are accepted by men. More than that, they have become so ingrained and entrenched in the culture it is almost impossible to have these definitions replaced. But it is desperately needed, as they are extraordinarily destructive to men in every way. They are at the heart of the explanation for why men are being taken advantage of every day and why so many are in such a poor mental state.

The first definition, as it relates to the subject, is what makes a man in America considered successful in their personal life.

Now, read this part carefully, and let it sink in, because this is really screwed up.

An American man sees his value as based upon the attractiveness of the woman that he can pull. Let's not forget that the term 'trophy wife' was coined in America. It's somehow become a symbol of success, capitalism, winning, and all the other great American traits. A hot wife is the ultimate reward in the American male mind.

So, a woman has become literally a trophy in the United States. To a successful man here, a woman is now another material item that you just pick up, like a Ferrari or a mansion. That's why men are willing to take something shiny, something that looks good – it's why in America, looks matter more than anything else. Now, I'd be lying if I said I haven't used my devilish good looks to my advantage in America, but that's not the point.

It follows, therefore, that a man doesn't mind anything a woman puts him through because her mere presence at his side shows the (American) world that he is successful.

It's a totally different mindset.

When I see a hot blonde woman in yoga pants with a Rolex watch walking three miniature poodles with a man next to her, I think about what a loser this man must be and what a pain in the ass the woman probably is. But most men in America look at the same situation with different eyes.... They think about what a winner this man is, ponder how successful he must be, and wonder how they can get one of these women.

It took me a long time living in America to realize this. But that's what it is. That's why men stay in these relationships. That's why they put up with it.

I know this guy, Jack, who had a very attractive wife. I didn't know them when they first got married, so I can't speak about the early years of their relationship. But I did know them both for the last six years of their union. In that period, from what I could see and from what he shared with me, his very attractive wife didn't care about him. She didn't cook for him, she didn't clean for him, she grumbled when his friends were coming over, she barely worked, and she didn't even sleep with him. She ended up leaving him – and they got divorced.

When I heard the news, I was happy for him, honestly. I celebrated his liberation. He could have done much better.

In fact, I was mystified why he hadn't given his wife the flick earlier – I could not see any way that she contributed to his life or how he benefited from having her around.

But now I understand why he took the divorce so hard and why he put up with an emotionally unavailable, financially draining, and physically unreceptive wife.

She kept him *looking* successful.

And today's American men have come to prioritize this mirage of success above all else.

Much to my chagrin, Jack still wears his wedding ring to this day. Super nice guy, but a hopeless beta who is victim to this wholly incorrect and wrong definition of success.

Many of you enjoy my famous Twitter stories, the factual retellings of my day-to-day life that have become viral sensations. Well, in one of them, I relayed the experience of turning up late to a date.

She didn't know, nor was it any of her business, but before I left to see her, I linked with some masculine guys at a private club to pregame. One thing led to another, and before you knew it, I was running a bit behind.

Once I managed to tear myself away from the bonds of male friendship, I opened up my phone to call an Uber. Unfortunately, there weren't many Uber Blacks in the area, and the estimated wait time was 20 minutes. I was tempted to call a standard Uber, which only had a wait time of 2 minutes, but decided to press on and wait it out. Thank goodness I did, too. Sliding into the back seat of a Mercedes GLE 350 after a wild afternoon with the boys just hits different.

We encountered a bit of traffic on the way across town, but I wasn't bothered. The car was comfortable, and "Born Free" by Kid Rock rang in my ears. I stepped out of the car and saw the sheila I was meeting. She was a fetching figure but wearing an unwelcoming expression and tapping her foot impatiently.

I let this young lady (who was and remains a very nice person that I really liked, but sadly didn't know any better) finish her diatribe and then asked her if she was finished. She said yes. I said, "OK – I'd like you to leave." She made the mistake of thinking that she, as the woman, held the upper hand.

When I sent this Twitter story post to one wealthy friend in his late fifties, he responded – *"I'm a bigger dick than you are, but I'd rather get laid."* Naturally, I laughed and called him a "cuck." His response? *"I'm married 37 years to a hot blonde."*

See what I mean about this warped definition? I'm married to a hot blonde, which means I am successful. That's all that matters.

When it comes to women, men in America think too big. I've got this hot blonde next to me... that's when they stop thinking. They don't think about her details or the small stuff that will make them painful, that could (will) cause them problems down the track.

Listen to me when I say this to you.

When it comes to women, men should think small. Because it's the details that are important – it's the details that will kill men. This is not something to play with. This is not something to take lightly.

The outcomes here are potentially life-altering and can destroy you emotionally and financially. You stand to lose all your money. You could lose your ability to see your children. More importantly, your children could grow up without you and end up more like Prince Harry than Tim Tebow.

As Dr. Jordan Peterson says, fix the things that you repeat every day that most people think are trivial. Your life partner has a huge role to play in these things.

Who cares how successful you think you look to others? That's not an alpha mindset. Which brings me to the first of *Nick's Rules*:

Success is a low-maintenance woman, not just a hot one.

Let me weigh in here with some alpha bluntness: *I'm sorry, fellas, but I don't care how hot you think your wife is. If she's high maintenance, you're a loser.*

In every other country and culture, if you have a high-maintenance wife, you are considered a failure. If you've got a bad wife – difficult or unpleasant – you're considered the dumbest guy around.

Success is a woman that listens to you, a family that respects you, and a personal environment where you are the leader. Living like a king is real success.

Be aroused by women that work hard for you and your children and are loyal to a fault – not for the ones with the best makeup and nails and biggest Instagram account.

I have had ex-girlfriends who couldn't believe that I was willing to let them go – and they would say to me – *you don't have anyone better, you're not going to get anyone better* – I didn't understand it at the time, but they thought that their only threat was if I found someone hotter.

But for me, it was never about that. I was more successful without them. In their mind, *they were my success.* These broads just couldn't work out why I didn't want them around.

So, I get that my message for American men is a big departure. What is right and what is popular are rarely aligned. Some may think I'm crazy, but people thought Noah was crazy for building the Ark too. And that's what I'm doing. I am building the ark for masculinity.

What is an Alpha?

The second definition that has screwed American men is even more destructive than the first.

Over the last two years, through all the hate that I have received, it has become abundantly clear that both American men and women have not the faintest idea of what being an alpha male is.

First, it is women who have defined what an alpha male is, and again, men have simply accepted it.

It's like taking dating advice from women. You never do it. You don't ask a fish how to catch a fish. You ask a fisherman.

The American definition of an alpha male works on the proviso that American men do not have a heart or a mind.

You see, everything within the alpha male definition created by women – height, weight, fitness, physical strength, gun know-how, military service, wearing a uniform, dress, presentation – it is ALL outside the heart and the mind – it is all physical and external.

This focus that has become so popularized means that it is commonly accepted that unless you are over 6 foot 2, have a six pack, can fight in a cage, run ten miles in under forty-five minutes, wear muscle shirts, have a massive appendage, drive a big truck, have calloused hands, and are unshaven, you need not apply for the status of alpha male.

Let me say this very plainly: **this is complete and total bullshit.**

This definition is not accurate. It's not correct. And it does not help you as a man at all. I need you, the young American man, to see that this definition is hurting you - that there is something inherent in the current definition of alpha that is not masculine.

It's a great irony, but perhaps not accidental, that the inverse is true for the definition (also conceived by women) of a pinnacle female. That definition is all internal. It's all mental. It's all heart. You can't judge an overweight woman. You can't judge a lesbian. You can't judge a woman who dresses like a man. It's all about 'go-girl', 'boss woman' mentality. You're not allowed to say that women should look a certain way.

But that's enough about women. **Let's get back to what really matters, alphas.** I'll admit, I have no idea how this definition of alpha male became so accepted in the United States, but if it was an orchestration, it's the best work of the modern woke feminists yet.

Chapter 2
Balls and Brilliance Will Get You Further Than Your Body

The Pulitzer Prize-winning playwright Archibald MacLeish in his play, "The Secret of Freedom" wrote:

"The only thing about a man that is a man is his mind. Everything else you can find in a pig or a horse."

Men, the battle in life is your heart and your mind. They are the muscles you need to train. They are the only functions that, when trained the right way, make you an alpha male.

You are not suffering externally and, by extension, physically. The opposite. You have been annihilated internally. It's your hearts and minds that have been captured.

No amount of time in the gym is going to help that.

It is true that if you are down or depressed, the gym is the best place to start. Healthy body; healthy mind. The more active you are, the better you will feel. There's something to be said about hitting the gym and getting yoked to impress the boys, but the emphasis on the physical when speaking about masculinity to men is so overdone.

It also only relates to a young man's alpha. The greatest alphas are alphas until their last breath. I don't think Winston Churchill, close to seventy years old when he took on the Nazis, could do many sit-ups. President Trump is an amazing golfer, but at 77, I don't think he is going to dominate a push-up contest the way he would have at 50. It's just a fact of life. The point is – these men's status as the ultimate alpha males cannot be questioned objectively by any reasonable person despite this – and that's because it's the heart and mind that counts. By the way, it's worth noting Napoleon Bonaparte was an alpha male who successfully took over a large part of the world, and he was tiny!

Even other prominent alpha king influencers surprisingly accept this female definition of alpha male, probably because it just happens to suit them or because they are telling an American audience what they *want* to hear instead of what they *need* to hear.

My father, the greatest alpha male I ever knew, would often say that the obsession with fitness was a version of political correctness in and of itself. *They want us all to be the same, look the same*, he would grumble. There is some truth to that. In fact, some might say that the most alpha position on this would be to not succumb to this almost universally accepted need to be in the gym and just be you. If you're built like a Greek god and can drive a golf ball 300 yards the way I can, that's great. But it's nothing to be ashamed of if you can't. It is the heart and mind that makes a man alpha.

There is nothing wrong with the gym, and there is nothing wrong with being physically fit, but you're a winner because you were born a man, not because you are going to go to the gym. Just by reading this book and being alive, you have already shown that what you are capable of within your own body is incredible - you beat one out of a billion sperm to get here, and somehow have made it to 18 or 25 years of age. You are literally one in a billion, and you're going to listen to some woman tell you that she doesn't want to eat what's in the fridge and wants to get takeout instead? Or put up with a woman that cracks it at you because you went to Kroger and bought the bread but forgot the milk? No.

Critically, and you need to let this soak in: there is no amount of gym that can make or help you lead a woman. Women fight you in the mind. They screw with your head. As a man, you can never become physically aggressive with a woman, so physical strength means absolutely nothing. You might be getting stronger to physically dominate other men, which God knows I enjoy doing, but your woman is battling you in the mind. I've seen 4ft 11 women utterly dominate 6ft 4 men.

The key to every human being's success lies in the mind. It is your goldmine between your ears.

Muggsy Bogues played basketball with more heart than Shaq. A short man can definitely be more masculine than a giant bodybuilder.

As my childhood friend in Australia, Garry Tuv says about being an alpha: *"It's not how you look; it's how you look at things."*

Masculinity is a mindset, not a physical feat.

A man is alpha because when he goes home, there is food on the table; he doesn't have to get takeout on the way home.

When he decides to ditch a couples game night his wife organized to play an 18-hole foursome with the boys at the country club, he isn't going to get a dirty look, listen to a lecture, or deal with sulking upon his return.

When he gets home, he doesn't get interrogated about his purchases.

When he comes home, there isn't a twenty-thousand-dollar couch in his living room that he has no idea about. There's not even a twenty-dollar cushion!

When he gets home, if she tells him she is feeling unwell and doesn't want to cook, he calls her out on it.

There are certain things that are off-limits for a woman not to respect. Family, food, and finances to begin with.

He has absolute control over these things because his ability to be strong is deep within him, and his wife knows it. He doesn't use it all the time, in fact, he prefers not to use it. But he is capable of it. Deep inside lies an ability to be very, very masculine. This ability is something that most American men seem to not even possess today.

What's the point of being and looking like a tough guy if, when you go home, you're not respected? What's the point of benching 250 pounds if you don't discipline your kids and your wife interrupts you and embarrasses you over dinner with friends?

The body part that you should focus on getting bigger – which is directly related to the heart, spirit, and mind – are your testicles.

When I think about all my friends that aren't married – they are all what I would call 'heart and mind' kind of guys. They are very strong in those departments. When I think about all my friends who got married the earliest, they are the weakest in their hearts and minds.

So, don't be focused on how you look and getting to the gym. Train your mind and increase the size of your testicles. That's where the fight is. That's where you will find your inner alpha. Women (often not even maliciously, it's their nature) and the world will continually come after your balls, not your abs.

Chapter 3
The Correct Definition of Alpha Male

There are a great number of different things that contribute to the makeup of a man that has an alpha mentality, spirit, and heart.

But there is one reality that underpins all alphas. Without this circumstance, you cannot be an alpha male. It's so important, it's even got its own rule. Are you ready for it?

An alpha male is never dominated by anything or anyone. He does the dominating.

Let's be clear: an alpha male is never dominated by anything or anyone, especially and including his wife. That is the correct definition of an alpha male, and that is the situation every man reading this book should aspire to.

If you are going to live your life as a male to your full God-given potential, you will be a slave to no one (save God). If you are a slave to your job, you are not living up to your full potential. If you have an addiction, you are not living up to your full potential. If you are governed by your children instead of the reverse, you are not living up to your full potential.

To put it in perspective, an alpha male goes to a woman to offer his strength, not get his strength. Here are some other common attributes or worldviews of alpha males:

- Alpha males are successful and not ashamed of their success.
- Alpha males are elite at what they do and strive for greatness.
- Alpha males always stick to their guns, they never back down, and they never apologize.
- Alpha males put their purpose (God, Trump, America, and greatness) above all else.
- America's standing in the world has been in decline since the moment the Left decided to begin oppressing alpha males.
- Alpha males speak their truth for all to hear, whether people like it or not.
- Alpha males keep women in check. The most dangerous women in the world (like Hillary Clinton, Taylor Swift,

Beyonce, and Meghan Markle) all have one thing in common: the lack of an alpha male influence in their life.

- An alpha male is not afraid to correct people when necessary, especially women. When an alpha male interrupts a woman to correct her, it's not "mansplaining." It's education.
- An alpha male is willing to make the tough decisions necessary to keep moving forward, like Tom Brady divorcing his wife.
- World history is the story of each country's alpha males striving for the greatness of their respective nations. America is the greatest nation in the history of the world because we were led by the strongest alpha males.

Some men look at this and believe that if they are alpha in every other way, except towards their wife, that still qualifies them for alpha male status. They say: *Well, she's the only person I change for, she's the only person I take crap from, she's the only person I allow to talk down to me. Everyone else I am tough with.*

NEWSFLASH: It doesn't.

I regularly hear the same thing about certain men when it comes to their children. *Oh, he's a real hard-ass, but when it comes to his kids, he's super soft, a total pushover.*

If you are a pushover with your kids or your wife wears the pants in your family, I don't care how tough and mean you are on the field or at work. You're not an alpha male. As a man and the leader of your household, your wife and your family represent you. So being as alpha with them as you are with the rest of the world is arguably even more important.

You see, masculinity never used to be political because it was overwhelmingly common. And frankly, it shouldn't be political. But in 2023, it absolutely is.

No masculine man has time for wokeness or politically correct ideology. How could they? It is anathema to the heart and mind of an alpha male. Do you really think drag queens would be reading to our children in public libraries if men were still stewards of the culture? Does anybody really believe that the use of pronouns would be as accepted and ubiquitous as it is today if real men still had a significant and substantial influence in the world? If masculinity was still prominent in our society, would so many still be wearing masks three years after a pandemic?

The Difference Between Alphas and Betas

Alpha males support:

- God & The Bible
- Law Enforcement
- Guns
- President Trump
- Capitalism
- Hooters
- Patriotism
- The National Anthem
- Crushing the establishment
- Traditional gender roles

Beta males support:

- Atheism
- BLM thugs
- Prince Harry & Meghan Markle
- Democrats/socialism
- Vegans/vegetarians
- Taylor Swift
- Liberal arts & humanities
- The New York Times & fake news media
- LGBTQ+ & gender pronouns

Quite the difference, isn't it?

That reminds me of a time I was seated on a flight across from a couple wearing masks. After I had made myself comfortable, legs spread wide apart, the husband leaned over and sheepishly requested that I put on a mask to sit near him.

He explained he was returning home to DC and was concerned about COVID exposure since he couldn't make an appointment for his latest booster shot before he departed for Florida. I was incensed. I told him to get bent and shamed him for even asking. His wife watched in awe as I tore her husband to shreds in the first-class cabin.

Once I had made it crystal clear that I would NOT be masking, he apologized and shrunk back in his seat, his eyes glued to the floor for the remainder of the flight. In the terminal, I came across the same couple again. The husband was, predictably, waiting in the Starbucks line while the wife was on the phone.

I overheard the wife talking to a friend in hushed tones. She was recounting the situation and said she had forgotten what a real man looks like prior to today. She mentioned how impressed she was with my powerful and authoritative demeanor. She told her friend she was having second thoughts about her marriage and wrapped up the call. We briefly made eye contact as I walked by. Even under her mask, her expression spoke louder than words. She was intoxicated by my masculinity.

Chapter 4
Alpha Males Hold Themselves (and Others) Accountable

Another critical aspect of alpha mentality is the support of personal responsibility. That's why an alpha king wants to oversee his own household and wants as little government interference as possible. In contrast, beta males support the government taking care of everyone because they have no confidence in their own ability and prefer a life without accountability.

An alpha king controls his family and ensures his children are in the best situation to be raised with the right values to endure the woke 21st century. The family of an alpha king will never embrace the woke, effeminate society the beta males are building. His family will always do the right things because he is the patriarch of the family, not the woke beta big government and media. An alpha king couldn't care less what Disney and Nickelodeon say. They aren't raising his children. Only beta males allow Hollywood and Washington DC to raise their children for them. Similarly, where beta males don't want to cause conflict with the school or teachers, an alpha king is outraged and disgusted at even the thought of drag queens reading stories to his children at school. An alpha male is someone who believes in Dictionaries, Bibles, and Constitutions for kids.

Betaness is treating all women with a special brush. You should always be a gentleman, but it is not a crime to be indifferent to women, overall, as a rule. As an alpha male, you only need to be really amazing and special to one woman in the world (female family members obviously excluded).

The concept that you must treat women as though they were an endangered species, and all angels, worthy of special protection, and that you must go out of your way to make sure you NEVER offend is just bullshit. First of all, it's not accurate, but secondly, it does nothing for your alpha mentality - it just forces you into "betadom." You do what's right for you.

I am continually amazed by the amount of men prepared to be punched in the face because they perceive that their girlfriend/fiancé/wife has been 'dissed' by another man, when that partner is controlling, disrespectful and often hostile to them. Not to mention that said partner may have been equally or more to blame for the circumstances leading up to her being insulted!

Let me explain something to you. What I am about to tell you is not politically correct, but it is the truth.

This isn't Hollywood. You're not playing some leading man. So, drop the hero complex. It's a complex that women want because it compels you to do things that are in *their* interests, but often against your own. You protect people, including women, that are worthy of protection. Women are not always right, and they aren't immune from saying and doing things that warrant criticism or challenging. You don't act defensive about a woman just because she's a woman. You protect a woman because she is in the right. You protect a woman that is a lady; just because she is a female does not make her a lady. Much like being alpha is a mentality, being a lady is as well.

I don't give a damn how unchivalrous that sounds; it's the truth. Now if you're married to the mother of your children, to a woman that is shy, that has never hurt a fly, that hates conflict and waits on you hand and foot – and something that you view as an 'attack' on her has transpired – that's different. Then you, as her leader, can choose to decide how you want to deal with it.

But to just reflexively want to throw punches on another man because he maybe had the temerity to tell your woman something she needed to hear – that you never had the balls to tell her – just because the culture has conditioned you that it's the right thing, is stupid. Protecting a woman that acts like a bitch to you at home and has continued the same behavior in public is weak, pathetic, emasculating, and downright dopey.

EGO – *Extraordinary Gonads and Overconfidence*

I never thought I would have to sell ego to men. I guess it is a sign of the times.

The feminized wokesters have been waging war on ego for eons. Men have been convinced that having an ego, being confident and exhibiting testicular fortitude is morally wrong. After all, doesn't the Bible preach humility? That pride comes before the fall?

Trust me, we are significantly beyond that point. Men haven't already just fallen; they've nosedived off the cliff.

Border on overconfidence; ego is your friend

Whatever you might think is noble, to me there is no virtue to being miserable, bossed around and walking around terrified of your own shadow. No ego equals no self-confidence. Overconfidence has a negative connotation, but things have gone so far in the other direction, I'd prefer a man to be overconfident than slink around with their shoulders slumped.

I'm here to tell you that the way to protect yourself as a man against any bad women is to operate with ego. That's the manly position, and the position that will mostly keep you out of trouble. Every man needs one, every man is born with one, and you are suppressing yours,

Some of you might be reading this, and thinking: *"What is Nick going on about? I have a huge ego..."*

I would submit that over ninety percent of you have become so accustomed to commonplace situations in the culture that you don't even realize you are operating without an ego.

Let me give you the most raw examples so you understand. Put YOUR ego aside and accept instruction from an alpha male at the top of his game.

If your girlfriend leaves you for another man, it is not normal for you to be friends with the ex-girlfriend and the new guy. Unless there are children involved, it is not normal for you to remain close friends with your ex-wife, like her Facebook posts about her girl's night out, or go and dress up in matching pajamas with her new husband and his kids.

Stop lying about it to yourself. Stop pretending. Think about it and be honest with yourself. Yes, it's very commonplace – but it is definitely not normal. You've just accepted these conventions.

Ego is self-confidence and a love of oneself.

It does not necessarily mean that you are better than other people, but it does mean that you are better than anyone that tries to hurt you. You're better than anyone who tries to put you down.

And American men have lost that. They let people talk down to them. They let people be nasty to them, and they have reserved a particular spot where women are allowed to do that. It's not just permitted; it's expected in many circumstances.

I had an experience with a bloke during a foursome not too long ago. We were about to make the turn when one of the boys started acting antsy. He was rushing his putting routine and ended up four-putting from 20 feet. When I asked him what was going on, he put his head down and said he needed to quit after 9 holes. He told me he was going to Taylor Swift's Eras Tour that night with his wife, and she would give him an earful if he played all 18 holes.

I put my hands on his shoulders and looked him dead in the eye. "The hell you're leaving this foursome with 9 holes left to play," I said. "Dial up your wife right now, and we'll settle this." Her response was, initially, quite nasty. But once I pumped him up with enough courage to lay down the law, her entire tone changed. All it took was him saying, "No, you don't understand. I am not asking you for permission to finish this foursome, I'm giving you the courtesy of informing you that I will be spending the next two hours with the boys." By the end of the call, she had been humbled and reminded of her role in his life, and it was smooth sailing after that.

You have been brainwashed that a woman is always right. That a woman can't be challenged. That you can't be verbally strong toward a woman. That you cannot put your wife in her place when she oversteps her place in your life. This has left men so confused. Their heads are all over the place. They are like Jell-o. They don't know how to behave or act, so they simply end up not doing anything.

It is even harder now, because of female expectations. I've been in relationships, where I have addressed something directly, and had her say: You're being rude. Why are you being so rude? And I've got to be honest with you – at the time, I thought I was being timid, that I was being quite soft compared to what I knew I was capable of and what I really wanted to say.

It's all in the mind. I mean, as patriotic Americans, most of us believe that if someone breaks into our homes, we should have the right to defend ourselves and our property. A man's home is his castle. Well, what about someone that breaks into your mind, as women often do with men? What about a woman who is mentally abusive? What are your rights as a man? Are you at least able to get up and walk out?

Today's man frequently has this strain of Stockholm Syndrome. They are stuck in these unhappy relationships, brainwashed into believing that this woman and this picture they have in their mind is more powerful than anything they can do on their own, and they don't want to lose them... so they just continue to carry the woman's bags. It's the tragic modern-day story of men.

Chapter 5
The feminization of faith, marriage, and the family unit

If you don't believe that there is a war on men, you really can't be a fair or objective person.

It is clear to any reasonable person that modern woke feminism and all other Leftist engines are bludgeoning men into relationships where the female partners maintain complete and total control.

It has been like this for so long that it's easy to forget that it wasn't always like this.

But it wasn't that long ago that we had the Greatest Generation. This generation was largely made up of alpha males living in traditional marriages where the men were in charge. This also happened to be America's golden era. Sixteen million Americans fought in World War II, and it hardened the men of that generation, molding alpha males who would set up the future success of America.

According to the Pew Research Center, the share of women aged eighteen to thirty-four that say having a successful marriage is one of the most important things in their lives rose nine percentage points since 1997 – from 28 percent to 37 percent.

Great news! Except... for men, the opposite occurred. The share of men voicing this same opinion dropped from 35 percent to 29 percent. Believe it or not, modern women want to get married. The trouble is men don't.

What accounts for the abandoning of men's desire to get married? The truth is that in 2023 there is very little incentive for a man to get married.

Men don't want to lose their freedom and wealth, just to be belittled and diminished by their significant other. In fact, thanks to de facto laws, you don't even need to be married these days to be fleeced by a woman.

Relationships are no longer appealing for alpha males, especially in a society where women are celebrated for having sexual partners with no strings attached. Alpha males can fulfill their sexual desires without getting into a long-term relationship that will chip away at their manhood.

As for marriage, I can tell you that even happily married men in their sixties are suggesting to young men in their twenties and thirties not to get married. I can think of at least a dozen that have personally told me that if they were young in 2023, they would not get married. It's not worth it. As my own father, married once for forty years to the same woman, told me three years ago – 'there is no upside for a man to get married in 2020.'

Get a prenup, or don't get married at all.

I'm often asked by my male followers that are thinking long-term about a particular lady what they should do. My advice is always the same: do not let her move in with you, and do not move in with her. You keep your place, and she keeps her place. Spend the night occasionally at her place, or she can spend the night occasionally at your place – but no more than that.

In the event, for whatever reason, you feel that you can't live with that situation, and you choose to move her in, from day 1, organize an arrangement with her where she is charged a nominal amount of rent (the amount doesn't really matter). But this is the best way to protect you legally from her coming after your money, as she will be considered a tenant as opposed to a de facto partner. Of course, it goes without saying, with all the collective experience of men over the last few decades, that if you do get married and you do it without a prenuptial agreement, you are an idiot.

Alphas, you must get a prenup. It's non-negotiable. If she doesn't want to sign it? See you later. There is no room for discussion. If she truly loves you, respects you, and is of good character, she will not hesitate. It can be a hard discussion, and you can expect pushback and, if you really like her, potentially heartbreak. But it is necessary.

Women Ain't What They Used To Be

I know that this is not going to be received well by lots of people, but I'm not writing this book to win a popularity contest. Here's the truth: women aren't women anymore. To say gender relations have changed dramatically is an understatement. Ever since the sexual revolution, there has been a profound overhaul in the way men and women interact. Men haven't changed much – they had no revolution that demanded it – but women have changed dramatically. In a nutshell, women are angry. They're also defensive, though often unknowingly. That's because they've been raised to think of men as the enemy. Armed with this new attitude, women pushed men off their pedestal (women had their own pedestal, but feminists convinced them otherwise) and climbed up to take what they were misled to believe was rightfully theirs. Now the men have nowhere to go.

Feminism is at its strongest in America, and sadly the change in behavior and attitude of American women has reflected that same magnitude. Don't take my word for it. Consider what are known as the "passport bros." For those unfamiliar with the term, it refers to American men who travel overseas to find love, having given up on the American dating pool because they believe there is a better chance of finding a traditional wife in other countries.

The internet is flooded with these men parading these foreign women, they say were raised to be wives. They dutifully cook for them, clean for them, and most importantly, respect and submit to them.

Men get female partners for three reasons - physical, emotional, and financial – and American women are often emotionally unavailable, financially a drain, which only leaves satisfying your physical needs. That's why a lot of people term it "recreational use only," like going to the gym.

I hear the complaints from thousands of my young male followers every day telling me: "*Mr. Adams, American women are being raised by women, they don't understand me, they are loud, annoying, needy, a pain the ass, they don't want to get along with my family, they don't want to have a family, they don't want to raise children the same way I want to raise children.*" So what else do you do with a woman like that, they ask me?

They answer their own question by going overseas, choosing not to get married at all, or limiting the pool to traditional women. Men deserve to be respected. Men deserve to be cared for. Men deserve to be allowed to lead. We want all these things. It's in our nature.

Faith

This is one of the reasons why liberals and feminists loathe Christianity. Church attendance is a non-negotiable part of any alpha male's Sunday. There's nothing the Left hates more than a father taking his son to church before hitting the golf course and watching football at Hooters.

They hate that the faith promotes traditional families and Biblical marriage, relationships where the man is the head of the household and the woman is subservient to the husband.

The problem is that people aren't going to church anymore, and traditional theology-centered lifestyles are disappearing. There is no question: the United States is becoming more and more secular. The most recent Gallup poll shows that only thirty percent of Americans attend church weekly, down ten percent from ten years ago.

To add salt to the wounds, far too many American religious leaders are weak, woke, and writhe with discomfort when having to engage with their congregations in meaningful ways.

The pastors of many big churches are not alpha males in the proper definition – they tend to reflect the hipsters and man-bun attitudes that increasingly define their congregation. Both the leadership and congregations of so many churches are more interested in being trendy, cool and informal rather than serious, adult, and alpha.

Let me be abundantly clear, churches with women or effeminate beta males in leadership roles that have cafes that serve soy lattes aren't real churches.

Chapter 6
Understanding The Nature of Sheilas

Again, I know that this chapter is going to cause a lot of outrage, but it is information, knowledge, and education that every man must be exposed to. And sadly, it isn't.

The female form will consume you if you do not assert yourself.

I don't say that to disparage women. I don't say that to justify men treating women poorly. In fact, quite the contrary. I just say it as a public service announcement for men. A nugget of wisdom from a man whose fandom of the female form is very well-documented, but has never allowed it to consume him.

It is true. Feminism has brought it out of women, amplified it, and made it more commonplace, but it was always there.

The nature of the female form is to take you over completely. I repeat: if you don't assert yourself, the female form will consume you.

If you accept that as a man to whom it is important that you be the leader, then you will assert yourself as much as you see necessary. Dominate is a terrible word with terrible connotations, and I don't want to use it. But if you do not lead your woman, she will lead you. It's just nature. It's like a lion coming across a dead deer – the lion will eat it.

Now, I must say that I grew up very differently from most Americans. I was raised in a Greek-Australian household in a very ethnically diverse area full of those old cultures I mentioned earlier.

I also went to an all-boys school, steeped in tradition, and very much in the British educational style – in many ways, what most Americans might consider a military school. It's why I am a big supporter of single-sex education.

My mother, and the mothers of my friends, were all women that had husbands that asserted themselves.

So from school to home to social settings, I never really came across women that didn't have a healthy respect for men or didn't accept men as their leaders. Therefore, I never saw the potential... until I came to America, and then I realized how different the genders are here. This upbringing, fortunately, made me more prepared to assert myself (although I'll be the first to admit I haven't always lived up to what I'm preaching either). It isn't easy, particularly when you feel very strongly about your female partner.

But I've noticed a particular fear in the men of the United States to be assertive with women. Which made me ask myself – why? Why does it seem so rare to find an American man that does assert themselves? It took a friend, Sanjay, in Australia to point out the reason to me. He said, *"Nick, they are the opposite of us. We saw it all around us. We were lucky to see it being done. American blokes have never seen it done."* And I started to realize that he was right. It is the reverse. Most American men have never seen it done. They've never seen a male assert authority over a woman. It was always their moms leaving their dad. Their aunts are leaving their boyfriends. It was always the man relegated to the doghouse, or sleeping on the couch, or kicked out of the house. Everything was always women complaining about men – mansplaining dad jokes, etc. It was always women asserting authority over men. It is quite a feat, I must say, that even through alleged victimhood, women have asserted their authority over men!

A question often asked of me is why it feels like the female form cannot be trusted.

That's a difficult question to answer, but I will say this. Just like any relationship, you've got to have it on your terms. Every interaction you have must be on your terms, otherwise it's on theirs.

This approach is not taken because you are a bad person. It is because you don't want a bad outcome. In the case of a female life partner, the types of potential bad outcomes include things like your children growing up without a father, experiencing a divorce, and losing your property. This is why strength and leadership are so important to avoid these potentially life-altering, devastating occurrences happening.

Family Unit

The concept of an alpha male is a traditional one. God created men first, and He did that for a reason. He gave us dominion over nature and appointed us the heads of our households. That's why the feminist movement was not only a rebellion against society; it was a rebellion against God and nature.

For that reason, all alphas believe that a child is best served by both a mother and father. That is the best condition for any child to be raised in.

Alarming statistics relating to children from fatherless homes:

- 63% of youth suicides are from single-parent homes.
- 90% of homelessness and runaway children are from single-parent homes
- 85% of children that show behavior disorders are from single-parent homes
- 71% of high school dropouts are from fatherless homes
- 70% of youths in operated homes are from fatherless homes
- 80% of all the youths in prison are from single mother homes

To further illustrate my point, I will rely on President Obama's words here from a speech he gave in June 2008:

"Children who grow up without a father are five times more likely to live in poverty and commit crime, nine times more likely to drop out of schools, and 20 times more likely to end up in prison."

This is not in *any way* to attack single mothers. Many of them do their absolute best given the cards they are dealt. And deadbeat dads are nothing but shameful betas.

The importance of a father's influence on a family is profound. It's the gravest of responsibilities. If an alpha king has children, they must be his number one priority.

An alpha male prioritizes his children over his wife.

Yes, an alpha male prioritizes his children over his wife. *Just like his wife should prioritize the children over him.* Being a parent is the most important role a man or a woman will ever have.

If an alpha king has married well, i.e., he is an alpha king, he will not need to devote any time to fighting with his wife or convincing her of his plans for their children – as this is valuable time that he could invest in and spend with his children.

The most common complaint I hear from young men today is that they feel that their girlfriend, fiancé, or wife deliberately tries to distance them from their own families – their parents, siblings, and best friends. This behavior ranges from making members of their family feel uncomfortable when visiting to outright trying to turn them against him. I once had a girl that, in an effort to lessen the likelihood of me visiting my parents while she was away over a long weekend, decided to uncharacteristically cook three days of food and put it in containers in the fridge.

There is not a more well-known example of this type of behavior, nor more successful, I might add, than the number of times Meghan Markle has done this to Prince Harry. Hence this commandment which I affectionately call the "Prince Harry Commandment."

An alpha male doesn't abandon his family, particularly at the request or desire of the woman in his life.

Every man's greatest fear is that their son will grow up to be like Prince Harry. Alpha males do not abandon their parents or families – they love them – they never do the 'Prince Harry.'

And while we are still on Prince Harry, let me spell it out because clearly, not even royals are immune: being alpha means not getting married if it requires you to surrender your testicles. Don't be weak and miserable. Life is too short. We've all met at least one nasty, gold-digging woman like Meghan Markle, Prince Harry was the guy stupid enough to marry her.
I used to like Prince Harry. He was born ten days after me. We went to similar schools. Prince Harry was a knockabout, cheeky lad with lots of personality – much like yours truly. He was just one of the boys. A man's man. Loved having a good laugh. Much more so, in fact, than Prince William.

But Prince William married perfectly, and Prince Harry chose horribly, making a life-altering, dreadful error.

He married the worst kind of American woman. Someone that is, in my opinion, manipulative, possessive, nasty, evil, and controlling. I think Prince Harry is miserable, and I doubt the marriage will last.

While I can't be certain, it is my belief that after getting married, Markle proceeded to try to separate Prince Harry entirely from his previous life. That meant turning him against his own family, friends, traditions, and lifestyle. She has been stunningly successful.

Look, I don't know the intricacies of their relationship – no one really does. But it seems indisputable that things went south with Harry and his family (without whom he is nothing more than another balding British bloke) since marrying this nasty woman.

Firstly, as a man (not to mention, a Prince!), he should be calling the shots, not her. She should be the one adapting to him, his family, and their ways. This is a woman that received everything a woman could dream of but continues to want it all on her terms. Why would you want to unite in one flesh with somebody that doesn't like your family or your ways and is trying to distance you from everything you know (your country, your culture, your upbringing)?

This, by the way, is a classic modern female social climber move. Markle knew and chose to marry into the royal family. She knew what accompanied that. But she decided to ignore the responsibility connected to that choice and convinced a weak Harry to go along with her. She turned a soldier into a wimp.

A strong man with real family values doesn't desert his family because of a new wife's influence (who doesn't have the same family values).

Anyway, the good news for Harry, and the good news for most of you young men reading this should you foolishly decide to do what he did: while he abandoned his family for a social climber, his family will be there for him when she is done using him.

No matter the provocation or circumstance, the moment your wife is directly or intentionally disrespectful to one of your parents, you should be searching Google for divorce attorneys that instant. If you don't, you're a beta. Every alpha male must have their limits.

Prince Harry is a cuck who takes his coffee with Splenda and almond milk. Don't make the same mistake he did.

Trust your wolfpack more than your wife.

If your wife or girlfriend or fiancé makes one of your friends feel unwelcome or uncomfortable in your home and you don't stamp it out, you should be at the closest Post Office within minutes, mailing your "Man Card" Express Post without a return address, because you're an embarrassment to men everywhere.

Your girl doesn't need to agree with every decision you make, but she should always respect your will. Also, and I have to say this, because this is endemic among men in the United States in their relationships – STOP telling your girlfriend or fiancé or special friend or wife or whatever she is – your secrets, your family's secrets or what your friends say to you. I know so many men in America that tell your girlfriend or wife EVERYTHING.

Talking and gossiping is a female trait. Yes, I know women love to know everything and the worst among them will give you a guilt trip about how there should be no secrets in a marriage, etc. Again, these are just efforts to control, that have zero benefit for you to comply with.

Resist the temptation to talk to your wife about your friends and your secrets. I know every marriage counselor in the country will disagree with me, but screw them – all the advice and rules dispensed tend to be in favor of the modern woman. Protect yourself and your friends. It is healthy and normal not to tell your woman everything.

Don't tell a woman everything. Some things in life should only be shared with your father, your brother, your son, and your butcher.

If you have a safe deposit box from before marriage, does she really need to know about it? Likely not. If you have a little bank account that you set up before you met her, she doesn't need to know. If you lend your brother money, she doesn't need to know. If your friend is banging his secretary, your wife should not hear about it from you. Locker room talk amongst your friends stays in the locker room. Don't go and share jokes your friend told you and the boys during a foursome that you know your lady will not appreciate. Smarten up, son! And if you make the mistake of thinking that selling the boys down the river to curry favor with a sheila to make her believe you are more enlightened than your buddies, rap yourself hard on your testicles to make sure they are still there!

Some things are only suitable for your inner circle. Your closest male friends, your brother, your father, or most importantly: your butcher.

A man's relationship with his butcher is sacred. There's an unspoken bond between an alpha male and the highly skilled tradesman he trusts to handle his meat. My butcher Mario and I personify that sacred relationship. We trust each other with secrets that will never see the light of day. He's a regular part of my foursomes and a great contributor to my scramble team because of his soft hands around the greens. Mario and I have bonded in ways very few others can understand.

Finding the right butcher for you can be tough. It can be exasperating. It can be painful. It can be exhilarating. It can be heartbreaking. Mario wasn't the first butcher I worked with. It took years of trial and error to find the right butcher *for me*, but it was worth the wait when I did. My point is this, put the same amount of effort, if not *more*, into finding the right butcher as you do into finding the right sheila. Marriages come and go. A relationship with a good butcher is forever.

If you want to make everyone happy, don't be an alpha male. Sell ice cream.

Being an alpha male in today's effeminate society is no easy task, it takes grit. Happiness must never be the goal. Greatness is *always* the goal.

If all you do is seek to make your wife happy, you will end up suffering. I'm warning you now, you'll never make a broad fully happy. No cap.

If all you do is seek to make your children happy, you will create monsters not good for the world, and you will be ashamed and unhappy (more on this in the 'discipline' section).

Betas prize happiness and no conflict; alphas prize success and will go through hell with a gasoline can to ensure it. Pain and suffering are always part of a great outcome. The struggle usually results in the best outcomes.

An alpha male leader should never try to be loved (that will come eventually from their family members) – it's better for them to be respected, even feared.

The most and best an alpha can hope for is contentment. When I look at my dad, he died a contented man. The same with the majority of my friends' fathers I grew up with.

Chapter 7
The Current State of America

I believe American men are more downtrodden than in any other country. That might sound like a pretty bold statement, but it's true. Estrogen is shoved in our faces at every turn. From feminist M&Ms to so-called "galentine's day," the United States of America has become the most feminized nation in the world.

It stands to reason that it is the hardest place in the world to be a man (but as we have discussed with wrong definitions, men don't make it any easier either). Now, of course, I am simply referring to the nation in relative peacetime. Of course, there are countries where war and infighting make it far more physically perilous for men.

But the United States is definitely the only place in the world where a man dressed as a woman can dictate what a man needs to celebrate at work, how he is able to speak to his family, and who reads books to his kids in the library. Put succinctly, it is the only place in the world where the strong man is weakened by the weakling dressed as a woman. That's pretty powerful.

Too scared or too nice

Since tribal times boys have been turned into men. A first slaughter, a first kill, a first trip to Hooters, a ritual or coming of age moment.

Men in Australia are similarly put through an initiation. It's unorganized. But it's everywhere. Your first rugby game. Your first punch up. The first time someone is rude to you, you decide to stand up for yourself and return fire.

What I have observed living here now for most of the last thirteen years is that *some* men in the US have never been initiated.

They never got the push. The smack. The leg thrown out by someone to deliberately trip you. The two guys who team up – one to push you, and the other crouched behind you to ensure you fall over when pushed. Pretty standard stuff in Australia.

So, in my observations, young men in the United States go either one of two ways:

1) They get scared of others, defensive, and allow insecurity to dictate their lives.

2) They think everyone is an angel and lose their killer instinct.

The key to masculinity is to be discerning. To have a sixth sense. An ability to identify clear and present danger – posed either by men, or in today's American society, probably significantly more likely – women.

More than that, men are also contending with a reality that the culture heavily favors females.

Every day online I come across gender reveal videos that show the mother visibly disappointed when the color is blue, not pink, with her commenting something to the effect of: "I really wanted a little girl." It's interesting because in all human history until now, and still in many other parts of the world, it's the opposite.

I don't believe it is a stretch to say that in general, these days, parents overshine or overemphasize the success of a daughter in a way they don't for their son. Nine times out of ten it isn't personal, just cultural. There is this leaning into the feminine, this trendiness – that is part of being in the in-crowd. For example, a daughter may not play softball as well as her brother plays baseball, but when she does, there is far more excitement, far more social media posting about it, the parents have even bought her a special pink mitt to use. My social media is full of men wearing t-shirts and caps donning the phrase – 'girl dad' – seeming to think that posting this photo and wearing this shirt is peak masculinity (I guess it is in America today!). Not to mention all the 'DADD' (Dads Against Daughters Dating) memes. Again, there is absolutely nothing wrong with being proud to have a daughter – the opposite in fact – but when the phrase and concept of 'girl dad' is so popularized and you barely see any reference to boy dads – you begin to notice. And I'm not the only one.

This has had a huge impact on boys over the last couple of decades, and it's been destructive. The boys have been neglected. Men have noticed that they are second-class citizens which has translated to a lack of confidence, and an emotional toll they take on their shoulders.

It is also clear that the feminized atmosphere within the United States leads to men who are masculine and that behave muscularly to being disliked and unreasonably viewed as bullies. Anyone who has any sort of strength is made fun of. If you call a woman out for something, you're an a**hole. You're a bully. You're being rude. You're a chauvinist. You're a tyrant. You are called every name under the sun.

The media also plays a significant role in propagating these effeminate concepts of leadership. For example, the way the media portrays Joe Biden as a strong, successful leader when he clearly struggles being coherent and falls over on stage frequently is absurd. It is particularly outrageous when on the other hand they regularly insinuate that Donald Trump is not strong, successful or leadership material, when all one needs to do is observe both.

During the 2020 campaign, on the very odd occasion Joe Biden left his basement and actually campaigned, I was shocked and disgusted simultaneously to see him consistently introduce himself this way:

"I'm Joe, Jill Biden's husband"

To borrow one of his own phrases, "C'mon, man!" You're running to be the leader of the free world, the Commander in Chief of the greatest military ever, the most powerful man in the world. Without Joe, as pathetic as he is, Jill Biden is NOTHING.

What weakness. How emasculated can you be?? Have you no pride, no ego, no sense of importance or significance? In history, at the time Biden was demonstrating this complete cuckery, there had only been 45 men ever to occupy this position. And yet, for a role so big-league, you define yourself by your wife. You're not asking people to vote for your wife. You're asking people to vote for you. People that rely on you, that need you to make their lives better and easier.

But the truth is (just like everything with Biden), he was being told to say this. That is to say, his people understood the female culture in the nation to the point where they knew that it was *in his interest* to introduce himself this way. That it was to his benefit to speak like this. How America has fallen.

I am continually amazed at men who I really like that have built their own empires – their own businesses – with value in the tens of millions of dollars (sometimes more), that fear their own employees, usually female. These men usually are talented, driven and certainly not stupid. But they have no balls. They have been castrated.

These employees represent them. These employees work at the pleasure of them. But even when they go rogue or they don't treat a client or customer or associate the right way, these men will not haul them into the office. They will not confront the problem head on. They will say, "Well, I've got to wait for the right time..." or "she's going through a tough time right now" – they will concoct any excuse to avoid directly dealing with the situation. I've never seen anything like it.

Why build an empire if you can't act like a king? Why pay people money if they won't do what you want them or need them to do?

The best part is – when a male client or associate brings it up with them – suddenly they find their masculinity (or think they do) and tell you that they don't appreciate being told how to run their business and that you can go and pound sand if you don't like it.

Always remember that being weak creates more problems in the long-run.

An alpha male deserves to be treated like a king

One thing I've discovered since coming to America is how little context American men have on how men in other parts of the world are treated.

A few months back, I was headed on a quick weekend trip to a tropical destination with a sheila. We arrived at the airport and pulled up to the valet. I quickly jumped out, tossed the keys and a $50 bill to the young valet, Antonio, and began walking towards the door.

"Um, hello?!," the sheila cried out angrily. I turned around to see her motioning at the trunk of my Jaguar. "The bags aren't going to carry themselves." I walked back to the trunk and pointed at the handles on my Titleist golf travel bag. "You see those? Those are handles for you to grab as you remove my golf clubs from my trunk."

She stared at me, dumbfounded. I snapped my fingers and called over Antonio. "Tone, son, you're a strapping young lad. Can you do me a favor?" I asked. "Of course, Mr. Adams," he quickly replied. "I'm at your service!"

Antonio is my go-to valet at the airport. He's a young chap, about 5'10, but very well-built. He's the type of guy you can tell who works out, clean-shaven with a chiseled jawline, piercing eyes, and tightly cropped hair. My big tips go a long way with Antonio; he's always on the ball, in my experience.

"Can you please demonstrate to this lovely young lady how to remove a bag from the trunk of my car?" He made quick work of my task, removing my golf bag, my roller suitcase, my backpack, and the sheila's carry-on. I passed him another $20 and motioned to the bird. "I'm heading in to get us checked in. Bring the bags up quickly, please."

I was met with complete silence. My instruction was not resonating, so I leaned in.

"Let me explain something to you, sweetheart. I am an alpha male," I told her. "I lead, you follow. You are the supporting cast, I am the main character. I am a king, and I expect to be treated like it. If you're not comfortable and capable of filling that role, now's the time for you to speak up."

"No," she shot back. "I'm a woman. I don't carry bags." That was it for me. I sighed deeply and said, "Alright then, have it your way." I informed her I was canceling her ticket and asked her to return my Jaguar to my house. She looked defeated and quietly nodded as I handed her my keys.

I called Antonio back over and explained the situation. He was very sympathetic to my plight and quickly offered to help me bring my bags in since he no longer had to worry about the car. I got to the desk inside and began the process of changing my trip. Despite my elite customer status, the bloke with the airline told me it was too late to get a refund for the broad's ticket.

"I'm so sorry, Mr. Adams. We could change the name on the other first-class seat, but our system simply won't allow me to process a refund." I told him I understood and had resigned to my fate. I pulled out my phone to send the woman a Venmo request for the ticket's cost, as Antonio crossed into my field of vision and sparked an idea.

"Antonio," I said. "Do you golf?" He nodded astutely. "Yes sir, I'm a 7.2 handicap," he said. "I'm not super long off the tee, but my soft hands around the greens keep me competitive."

I pondered for a moment. "Cancel your weekend, son," I said with a twinkle in my eye. "You've just got yourself invited on the golf trip of a lifetime." I sent the Venmo request anyway (it covered the cost of Antonio's tee times) and returned to the desk to have the other first-class seat assigned to the young and masculine valet.

We boarded our flight and took off. When the stewardess arrived with my ice-cold domestic beer, she excitedly said she had a surprise for me. "We saw your name on the passenger list this morning, so I made sure we had something special for you," she said. "We're serving filet tonight. Prepared just the way you like it."

She hurried away, and I turned to Antonio. "Have you ever had a flight like this, my boy?" I picked up my domestic beer and looked down at the napkin. A phone number was scrawled across the corner. I took a sip, spread my legs wide apart, and roared, "This is the way of an alpha male."

The denial of sex by the male is the most alpha act

Everyone knows that all men love, crave and desire sex. What's the old saying? A man thinks about sex every seven seconds. It's true.

But American men are on another level. In all the different cultures I have been exposed to, I've never come across the American male approach to sex. I think it's because they've been raised with a lack of discipline.

Again, I am unsure of why it is like this, and this is only a generalization based on many conversations with friends and followers, but American men can sleep with a woman no matter how they are feeling towards her. I've heard stories of American friends sleeping with women that have stolen money from them, won't let them see their kids, who have sworn at their parents and don't let their friends come over.

The most fascinating part is that when I have had a direct conversation with buddies about it, they proceed to tell me being able to treat sex as a physical act without emotion (i.e., not even liking her) is the most male or alpha you can be – it's like being in the jungle, they tell me. What?! I can't make this up.

This is yet another example of American men having some concept in their mind about masculinity and gender relations that is completely wrong, to begin with, but more than that, something that greatly weakens their position in the pursuit of the real alpha male mentality. It doesn't take you being a man to have sex. It takes a man to **not** have sex.

For those who are uninitiated, let me explain something to you. Women use sex to get their way. It is often used as a tool of manipulation. Let me tell you how it's done. Woman says a really offensive thing she knows has personally upset you. Then twenty minutes later, she starts rubbing the back of your arm, and before you know it, you're doing it like they do on the Discovery Channel. Imagine how much this must have happened to poor Prince Harry. It's manipulation 101.

I'll give you an example. A few years ago, I was seeing this bird who had started to get too comfortable with me. One day it all came to a head. She brought back the wrong type of yogurt for breakfast (I only eat full-fat Greek yogurt). I was deeply bothered by this, so naturally I corrected her, but she was less than enthusiastic in her apology.

Later that day, she slammed my car door, not intentionally, but the delicate electronics housed within the car door didn't care about the intent. I exploded on her, issuing a correction that rattled her to her core. After that, her apology was, shall we say, more enthusiastic.

She cooked me a steak dinner, a 32oz t-bone steak, if I recall. I refused to budge, continuing to give her the cold shoulder all evening. After dinner, I left her with the dishes and headed upstairs to the theater room to watch the Trump rally to decompress for the night.

About half an hour later, she walked in and sat next to me and tried to cozy up. "The dishes are all done and put away, Nick," she said. "I brought you some dessert." I accepted the baklava, which is when her intentions became clear. The tone of her voice changed, and she began to make her move, but I quickly stopped her. I was still stewing and, frankly, the thought of intimacy with her was the furthest thing from my mind at that moment.

"Excuse me, President Trump is about to speak. This is not the time for this," I said, sitting up and gently removing her arm from mine. "I think it's best if you go home, I'd like to watch the rally without any distractions."

I ended the relationship the following day, because the yogurt incident showed me that she was not a detail-oriented person. But I did so on my terms. I didn't allow her to seduce me into an undeserved forgiveness. I made sure she learned her lesson.

If a woman behaves in a way that is unacceptable, we (I include myself in this) lose the desire to be intimate with that person, at minimum, for that day, but usually longer. I think it is true that most men are not aroused by a dominating woman, contrary to whatever sexual fantasies they might occasionally harbor. They are aroused when they are the leader.

Remember that the absence of leadership is the beginning of the end. It's the beginning of your pussification and becoming her 'bitch.'

Chapter 8
Alpha Males Need Assets, Not Liabilities

Every male in a relationship must ask himself – what does she do for me?

I believe every man should be a protector and a provider, but no man should ever be so invested in being in those roles that he is not awake to the fact that the woman in his life is doing nothing – other than taking. As my father would always say, you need a woman that will compliment you. That will add value to you.

What does she do that makes your life better? I'm not talking about money. Maybe she inspires you, maybe she calms you, or maybe she joins your company and is a great employee. There is nothing better than a family business with which both of you are in. But she has to offer you something. Otherwise, there is no point. She can't just take.

I happen to be in a very fortunate position where, materially, I have everything. I work incredibly hard and have reaped the rewards of that hard work, something that is only possible in America. So, I am only looking for someone to make my life better, for a contributor in the ways that I need. Even if you aren't in that position, that is the mindset and attitude you must adopt.

Everyone is different in what they seek. But for me, the most important thing, I think, is peace. You want a partner that brings you peace. A woman who will bring you an ice cold domestic beer and shut the hell up for an hour after you get home to let you unwind. That's the rare kind of woman who can make your world more peaceful.

Sometimes a woman will start off benefiting you, and then stop. It's perhaps best exemplified by women who show themselves to be a completely different person until they are engaged or married, at which point they change, because the dynamics of the relationship have changed.

But there may be other situations, too, where women change while in their relationship with you. Here's what you need to know: the moment a woman no longer benefits your life, or wants to be agreeable to your expectations, or disrespects you, that's when you immediately stop your generosity. That's when you no longer give.

If you continue to allow her to benefit from who you are as a man, you become a sucker. But, the reverse is also true.

If you are lucky enough to have an amazing woman that cares for you, loves you, protects you, puts you on a pedestal, and adds value to you, giving her a great life does not make you a sucker.

You *should* give a woman like that the best possible version of life. She deserves it.

Alpha males just say NO to the snip

There are some really odd trends in the United States pushed by women.

I'll never forget driving on I-35 in North Texas and seeing a billboard advertising vasectomies for men. Then in the same week one of my buddies my age told me his wife had mentioned it to him, and another one of my older tennis friends, aged 70, openly told me he had had a vasectomy twenty-five years ago. I remember coming home, and thinking, "What a bunch of pussies!"

How on earth is it that men are getting the snip, limiting their reproductive options, while women are freezing their eggs to have more reproductive options? Wake up, gentlemen. You are being played. Next time you board a flight you may as well store your man purse in the overhead bin.

If you let a sheila convince you to get the snip, you deserve to get cleaned out in your impending divorce. Not only is it demoralizing, demeaning, and inhumane, it is strategically unsound. What if the world needs to be re-populated someday? Someone will have to step up. It would be a shame if you couldn't participate!

The most successful alpha males are not ostentatious

Do you remember the false definition of alpha male? The one written by women, where it's all physical?

The extension of this false exterior definition is this idea that in order to be an alpha male you have to own eight Lamborghinis, a Rolls Royce, a private jet, a yacht, wear a Rolex, and smoke expensive cigars.

Now, don't get me wrong. I am incredibly successful. I own a sports car, live in a mansion, have more awards and accolades than I will ever know what to do with, smoke high-quality cigars, and sport a very expensive pair of Oakley's, but that's not what defines my masculinity.

I love luxury, and I applaud anyone that has reached a level of success in their life that allows them and their family to have and enjoy these things.

But they are not necessary to be an alpha male.

There are lots of alpha males driving around in Nissan Pathfinders and Hyundai Tucson's that don't wear designer suits with Armani sunglasses, and have never smoked a Gurkha Royal Courtesan Cigar, let alone any cigar.

In fact, I would say, as a rule of thumb, the most successful alpha males in the world are not ostentatious. They go out of their way to fly under the radar, and not show-off or attract notice. (Of course, I am different because I am in a public position and I've inspired an international movement to restore men to their rightful place at the forefront of society, so those rules don't apply to me!)

Confident humility is a core trait of an alpha male. Being humble isn't enough for me. A lack of confidence is too often confused with humility. I have worked tirelessly to become the most humble man in the world. I have to be the best at everything I set out to accomplish, including humility.

A man that cares more about his Jordans than his bank account cannot be an alpha

An important note: if you can afford the greatest things of life, and you love luxury (as alphas tend to), and you are doing it for yourself and your family, that's fantastic. All power in the world to you.

But if you can't really afford it, or you can afford it but are buying these things to impress blonde bimbos, or attract women, that's a beta mindset. It's also childish. There is a difference.

Ostentatiousness aside, appearance is important. As an alpha, you don't need to be wearing a $25,000 tailored Italian suit.

But you do need and want to be taken seriously. It's often forgotten that an alpha is an adult. They typically aren't interested in being trendy or youthful. You need to have a certain air of gravity, a seriousness – that you are a serious person not to be disregarded or played.

Dress more "daddy," less dad.

You should always be clean, well-presented, and dressed nicely. You don't need a lot of money to be able to do this. A nice crisp business shirt, pants, sports coat, and polished dress shoes are your friend.

Have you ever seen Donald Trump in ripped jeans and a t-shirt? Of course not. On God, a man that wears skinny jeans cannot be masculine. Can you fathom seeing Roger Stone out on the town in joggers and a tank top? Nope.

An alpha male is a serious person and must dress accordingly. Why do you think Donald Trump is always the best-dressed and most handsome man in the room? Style is confidence, and your presentation tells others a lot about who you are.

Being an alpha male is like being a General. You never see a General with a dirty uniform. You never see a General holding his wife's hand during a parade. You never see a General asking to not be woken up during a Code Red. He doesn't say: 'let me get my pumpkin spice latte.' He throws his wife out of bed, takes the call and gets down to business.

Body language is important, as it reflects your mind and spirit

I often see young men walking at the gym, and I feel like telling them *"Always walk like you mean business."*

Countless people have told me, "Nick, you have this certain air about you. It's like people can feel when you're about to enter a room, and the attitude of the room completely changes." The aura of masculinity that precedes me is not only an indicator of my elevated testosterone levels, it's a reflection of my body language.

Body language is much more important than your body because it tells the world what you think of yourself, and what you see as your place in the world.

I distinctly recall one year at an end of year assembly in elementary school, I won a prize, and was called before the school to collect it. When the assembly was over, I walked out to find my father furious.

"When you go and collect an award, or you walk to the front of the room, you don't walk up there with your head buried in your shoulders, like you're ashamed or embarrassed. You stick your head up, set your shoulders back, and walk up there like you own the place."

On the flipside of this, we have the "Disney adult." If you've opened up Facebook, you've likely seen what I'm talking about. A man with his wife/girlfriend at Disney, wearing matching t-shirts and mickey mouse ears. It's the look of a broken man. Shoulders hunched forward. His face plastered with an artificial smile. He's lying to himself and to the world when he says he's having a good time. He doesn't want to be there. You can see it in his eyes.

When I see posts like this, I report them for abuse and slide into the man's DMs. I invite him for a private one-on-one meeting at Hooters. It's my obligation as an alpha male to help these sad blokes out. Sometimes these meetings prove effective. Other times they don't. But even just one man that I can spare from a life of subjugation and cuckery at the hands of Mickey Mouse and his female foot soldiers is worth all the time, energy, and money in the world.

Alpha males don't take unnecessary risks with their lives.

An alpha male is the leader of his tribe, and irreplaceable.

That's why it is irresponsible for men to take unnecessary risks, as the consequences from a freak event don't bear thinking about it. Did Winston Churchill ever ride a roller coaster? I don't think so.

'Roller Coasters' here is more of a euphemism, but the point remains. If you have a family, and as the leader of the family, you should not be skydiving or BASE jumping or BMX bike riding. If something happens to you, they will lose their leader, or they won't have their leader at full capacity for some time, and you can't afford that.

Now, I have spoken with the President many times, I have been branded as his favorite author, after all, and we've never discussed this. But we've all wondered why President Trump chose to make his mark on the world of business instead of the world of sport. He was world renowned for his skill in football, baseball, soccer, golf, and numerous other sports. This principle is why, I speculate, President Trump never pursued professional athletics. He knew his calling was higher than sports, and opted to become a billionaire and president rather than risk his health on the gridiron or the baseball diamond.

You don't only represent yourself – you fight for the people in your life that matter to you. Your friends, your family, the children of your friends, those that have been loyal to you. Don't be reckless. Be smart.

Alpha males are servant leaders; they don't just fight for themselves - they fight for their tribe.

Anyone who follows me on Twitter knows that I cop a lot of hate. By the way, just so you know, I revel in their hate. I drink feminist tears like an ancient warrior drinks the blood of his fallen enemies.

But it doesn't change the fact that I have become one of the most hated men in the country. One of my favorite lines of attack of these Twitter trolls is when they tweet a million variations of 'you sure whine, complain and cry a lot for an alpha.'

This is a trap the devious feminist left love to set.

In a piece of what can only be described as evil genius, they use the definition they created of the big burly stoic man to protect themselves or any action they support from any criticism or complaint from the strongest in society.

Better put, this is how they stop a man from leading. They say, *"Well, hold on, to be an alpha, you can't whine about it being hard to be a man in society. That's not very alpha of you."*

They want you to suffer in silence. They don't want you to speak out. They want to muzzle you and subjugate you. So they make fun of you – they try to gaslight you into questioning your masculinity in a bid to stop you from being masculine.

For the record – being an alpha is VERY much about correcting those in need of correction and leading by speaking out about the issues.

An alpha male refuses to be disrespected, and will let his displeasure be known

But, Nick, aren't alphas supposed to be stoic? Isn't that Alpha Male 101?

Yes, part of masculinity is being stoic; there is no doubt about that. For your wife and your children, you need to be a rock. For example, you should go out of your way to conceal your pain and worry about serious internal family matters such as health and

45

finances – because if you do – the fact that the strongest person is frightened will only worry them about the situation more.

But when it comes to most other things stoicism is weakness. If your son walks into the kitchen and joins the breakfast table without so much as saying "Good Morning" to the others already seated, it's not time to be stoic.

If you go to a Parent Teacher evening and are told that your daughter is disrupting the class and learning of others, it's not time to be stoic on the drive home.

If you haven't eaten all day, and your stay-at-home wife has not prepared anything for you to eat and is sitting on the couch watching "90 Day Fiance," it's not time to be stoic. It's in fact time to be emotional. To be passionate.

If not given the treatment they deserve, alpha males should not hesitate to let their displeasure be known and demand better.

Being an alpha means you are bothered by so-called little things, because if those you love and those in society can't get the little things right, they may as well not even try for the big things.

If you're waiting on me and want a good tip, don't call me anything other than "sir." I don't want you to joke around with me and get cheeky. I want you to keep the beverages flowing and show me the respect I'm entitled to as an alpha male. That's it.

An alpha male is never afraid to send his food back to the kitchen or ask to speak to a manager. Ever.

As a man, you are a force of nature. You don't just deserve respect, you demand it by your mere existence. You aren't more of a man for not letting things bother you and suffering; you're a man for setting your expectations and enforcing them to the extent they are in your control. Alpha males aren't entitled. They're deserving.

Let me tell you a story that illustrates this rule. A few months back, I had a run-in with some beta males, who didn't give me the respect I deserved when I went to pick up a rental car for a boys' trip.

Things got off to a rough start when I walked in and was greeted by a thin young man with a dark mustache and black-painted fingernails. "How can I help you today, bro?" he said. I stopped dead in my tracks and looked him up and down. "Excuse me," I shot at him as my posture stiffened, "what did you just call me?"

He repeated his greeting, slightly perplexed, and then I exploded. I asserted my masculinity by berating the slender young man in front of the entire store. "You are NEVER to refer to me as anything other than 'sir' or 'Mr. Adams,' do you understand that?" I told him. "You will give me the respect I deserve, or you will feel my wrath."

Before I could even finish, the man was practically on his knees, begging for forgiveness. He was shaken to his core. He was quivering like a scared puppy in the shadow of a roaring alpha male. Just then, a charismatic latino manager smoothly stepped in and attempted to lower the temperature of the situation.

Alejandro offered me a hot black coffee as a peace offering and began working to get me into my full-size SUV and on my way. "Senōr Adams, I have good news, and I have bad news..." he said. "We, unfortunately, don't have the Suburban you ordered, but I have something better for you we're going to get you into at no additional cost."

"My life is in your hands, amigo," I said. "Don't let me down."

"I have a 2023 Mercedes EQS SUV for you—tons of horsepower. One of the coolest cars I've ever seen, and it's fully electric!" he said with misguided excitement. His words were met with a masculine stare so icy the Arctic ice temporarily expanded.

"Sir? Does that car work for you?" He said tentatively. "No, Alejandro, that car does not work for me," I replied. "I don't 'do' electric cars, and I'm insulted you would think I would be amicable to that kind of vehicle." As I carried on my verbal barrage, I noticed the well-groomed manager was wearing an engagement ring.

I finished by telling Al to "get bent" in no uncertain terms. The entire facility had briefly fallen silent and still after my tongue-lashing. But after a moment, the room tenderly began to come back to life, and I looked back to the manager.

"Well, what's your plan to do right by me? Where's my car?" I prodded, much calmer but still irritated. Alejandro assured me he would find the perfect vehicle for me and asked what I wanted in a car.

"Internal combustion SUV. I need room for four guys to sit with their legs spread wide apart and enough space for a 46" tour stiff Fujikara driver shaft." I said. He rushed away and returned about 15 minutes later with the news that a manager from another location about an hour away was en route with a brand new black

GMC Yukon XL, and he was doing double time to get it to me ASAP.

"That will do, son," I said as I gave him a firm pat on the back. "But I want the Mercedes too. You aren't going to pawn that ticking time bomb onto anyone else."

Alejandro nodded his head and went back to draw up the paperwork for the electric SUV. After I signed it, Alejandro gently grabbed my arm. "I wanted to tell you face to face that I submitted my resignation letter right before I brought you your paperwork. I'm not cut out for this, sir. I have been living a lie. You opened my eyes. I'm still a boy. You are a man. This is a job for a man."

I told him I appreciated his kind words and took the keys. I stopped beside Alejandro and rolled down the window while driving off the lot. "Hombre, here, take this," I said as I extended him a business card and locked eyes with the man. "Email me if you ever want to play a round of golf when you grow up."

I can't speak to any specifics, but what I can promise you is this: I made certain that this particular electric vehicle will never see the light of day again.

Remember, an alpha male doesn't just 'go with the flow' when things don't go his way. The flow goes HIS way. Always.

To put a pin in this conversation, let me say this without any stoicism – and just pure passion: We define what it means to be an alpha male, not them.

Consider marrying women from cultures that respect and honor men

I wasn't in the United States in 1982 (not even alive, in fact), but I must believe that when men were giving their hamburger orders to waitresses that year, they were not asking for their hamburger to have 'no tomato', 'no onion' or 'no lettuce' (insert any other ingredient!).

I also have to believe that very few were professing food allergies or informing their fellow diners and waitresses that their stomach doesn't agree with (insert ingredient).

I'm pretty sure they just had to decide how they wanted their burger cooked, and if they wanted it with cheese. That was it.

Similarly, there were only two kinds of coffee – black, or with cream. (*For the record, I drink mine black and hot, just like I like my women sometimes!*)

I don't do Starbucks (I've been boycotting them for some time), but when I overhear others describing their coffee orders, my head wants to explode. An iced, half-caff, Ristretto, Venti, 4 pumps, sugar-free, cinnamon, dolce soy skinny latte? The world has gone mad.

Not even mentioning almond milk, oat milk, cashew milk, oak milk... what happened to good old fashioned regular milk? It was bad enough to get the reduced-fat (2%) and low-fat (1%) versions – but all the other milk options of today? Crazy.

This obsession with phony milk is an insult to God and nature. Under no circumstances will I ever allow a drop of it to pass my lips. If you want your son to grow up to become like Rory McIlroy or Dylan Mulvaney, go ahead, give him a glass of almond milk. But if you want your son to grow up to be worthy of carrying your last name, you'll banish these satanic beverages from your household right now. God gave us cows for a reason.

I remember a time when I was asked if I wanted "oat milk" in my coffee. I informed the girl behind the counter that it's not physically possible to milk an oat and immediately left. I liked that coffee shop, but I haven't returned since that day. I refuse to support a business that feeds into this new age feminist milk rubbish. Men have to take a stand.

But that isn't all. Peanut allergies were certainly not in the mainstream public discussion, nor were food allergies of any other kind.

Yet, if you go to California, and I love California (the state, not the politics), I challenge you to find a person of any of the 57 different known genders that does *not* have a food allergy. I'm exaggerating, but you get the point.

Everyone has something wrong with them now. It's cool to have an allergy. It's perfectly acceptable, almost laudable, to not eat something.

Of course, everyone has preferences. Of course, you have the freedom to eat what you order and pay for exactly the way you want it. I am not disputing either.

But I am observing that something very significant has changed since 1982. That year, by the way, is completely random. I could have picked 1978 or 1987 or many other calendar years.

So, what changed? How did all of this become so mainstream? The only conclusion I can reach is that it is all a product of female-led culture.

Pickiness or fussiness is a female trait. My theory is simple: pickiness began with women, infiltrated male culture, and now it's normal for a man to ask for a salad with no cucumber, or a coffee with almond milk instead. Not only is that effeminate, it's also unhealthy. Giving an alpha male coffee with almond milk is like filling up a fighter jet with unleaded regular gasoline.

Businesses and the health industry adapted to this new norm, and we are where we are today. There is no other explanation as to why this didn't happen in 1982 and it does now. It must be the result of females getting more influence on the culture. The timing is too coincidental.

As for the allergies, it reminds me a lot of what Bill Maher said about gender dysphoria on his *HBO Real Time With Bill Maher* show:

If you attend a small dinner party of typically very liberal, upper-income Angelinos, it is not uncommon to hear parents who each have a trans kid having a conversation about that. What are the odds of that happening in Youngstown, Ohio?

If this spike in trans children is all-natural, why is it regional? Either Ohio is shaming them or California is creating them.

It's like that day we suddenly all needed bottled water all the time. If we can't admit that, in certain enclaves, there is some level of trendiness in the idea of being anything other than straight, then this is not a serious, science-based discussion, it's a blow being struck in the culture wars using children as cannon fodder.

It's the same with allergies and pickiness in the United States. Either everyone had allergies and suppressed them, or didn't breathe a word about them.

For the record, real men eat just about everything. The only mandatory fussiness for an alpha male on this subject is quality of food. Alphas should always eat the best of the best. High quality food. If a girl doesn't eat steak or seafood, run!

I'll close this with a funny anecdote. A friend who I grew up with, a true alpha male in every sense of the word, has two children, both with severe nut allergies. He was telling me about this, how common it was in his children's schools, and asked me to please be careful with the chocolate I was preparing to buy for them on my upcoming visit. I asked him if he ever wondered how no one in our grade or school that we knew of had such allergies when we were at school and yet now so many kids have them?

His answer has me laughing to this day. He said, "Oh, mate, I had 'em. 100%, I had allergies but they were all cured by my grandmother." He asked, "You know how?" I said, "How?"

"When the doctor told her what ingredients I was likely allergic to, she said no worries, Doc, I'll deal with it. Don't worry. And we'd go home and she'd force feed me food with those ingredients. It almost killed me a couple of times, but guess what? No allergies now!" Knowing his grandmother and her vintage, I'm inclined to believe him!

Exceptional in a different way

When I first visited the United States over my first few trips, I thought this was the most masculine nation in the world. I remember walking through sections of Hobby Lobby dedicated to man caves, sports, cars, garages, and I remember thinking how great it was that men were catered for specifically. I'd never seen these kinds of items available in any other nation in a regular chain store.

But over the years, I realized it was all a show.

The first penny to drop was when I understood that the very concept of a man cave, much like the definitions of a man and alpha male, was a construct of the female. Think about it. In a home purchased (in all probability) mostly through the income of the man, only a tiny sliver of the home is dedicated to that man. The female gets ninety-five percent of the house (she can only do better if she divorces him... joke... not really), and he gets five percent of it, even in cases where a female has contributed nothing on the right side of the decimal point. Not to sound like a modern day woman or anything – but surely at least fifty-fifty is fair?

A man cave is nothing more than a cage, created by women, to contain a man's natural masculinity. These broads view us like dogs. Our masculine tendencies are bad behaviors that need to be contained by a kennel – aka "man cave."

Let me be perfectly clear, my entire house is a "man cave." My masculinity cannot be contained to just one room. I will never allow a woman to tell me that I can't have a golf simulator in the living room, or that I can't have my Hooters swimsuit calendar in the kitchen, or that I can't have my recliner directly in front of the TV. I'm fine giving her a room that she can decorate the way she likes. A small area for her to do her scrapbooking or host her sewing machine. But my house is my castle, and a man has every right to set it up how he sees fit. If a sheila doesn't like that, she can get bent and find somewhere else to live. I am an alpha male. I will NOT be put into a cage.

The ruse was completely over when it dawned on me that there is something unique in the masculinity space in the United States.

It's the only country in the world that has outsourced masculinity. It's the only country in the world that provides an outlet for masculinity. Let me explain.

In the good ole USA, you can go shooting with the boys, play paintball, go to Hooters, Twin Peaks, Tilted Kilt, find an automated batting cage, or visit Top Golf. The opportunities for an outlet of masculinity are everywhere. Sounds like a great thing, right?

Except when you realize the culture has been set up in a way that these are the only places where you are supposed to be or 'allowed' to be masculine. It's basically saying: *"When you come home, you're with me. You're mine. Go and be a man there, not when you come home to me."*

Juxtapose this with men from other countries, where it's the opposite. Men are men everywhere. Not only given situations.

Again, not uncoincidentally, being feminine in the United States is not outsourced. I've never heard – don't store all your clothes here, go and get a storage unit. Or don't use this kitchen, cook it outside and bring it in.

I love Steve Harvey. I am utterly inspired by his life journey, grind, charisma, and approach to life. Like all the greats, Mr. Harvey's life is marked by great loss and great victory.

He was homeless, endured two divorces, and an unscrupulous accountant almost ruined him financially. To me, he is the personification of resilience and relentlessness.

The thing I am most fascinated by is that while most see Mr. Harvey as only an entertainer, he is also a great businessman. The popularity of *Family Feud* in the United States has led it to become a worldwide franchise, with over 50 adaptations outside the United States. Not many realize this, but Mr. Harvey now owns the *Family Feud* franchise globally. Now that's true business genius!

On a personal level, I am extremely moved by his dedication to his parents, even in death. He has noted several times in interviews that he still strives to make them proud, and hopes they are up in heaven looking down on him happily. These are sentiments I can very much relate to. I know that I still live for my father even though he is no longer with us, and that my mother is my everything.

But perhaps the story that makes me most admire Mr. Harvey is the one regarding his teacher.

A very young Steve Harvey wrote in class on a piece of paper that he wanted to be on TV. His teacher ridiculed his dream. After he fulfilled his lifelong goal, every year this teacher was still alive, Mr. Harvey would send her a TV for Christmas, because he wanted her to see him, each of the seven days a week he is on!

This is what anybody, who has been ridiculed and doubted, dreams of being able to do. I can more than relate. Many of my teachers were doubters, not to mention others!

But when it comes to the subject matter of this book, while obviously I've never had a chance to sit down with him and speak about any of it in-depth, it would appear he and I have a big difference of opinion. He says:

Marriage is not 50/50. It has never been 50/50. It will never be 50/50. I'm gonna hold up a card and I'm gonna show you what marriage is. Marriage is 85/15. 85 to the woman and 15 to the man. Let me explain something to you. The reason a woman is in charge of the house is because they know more about it. They know the kids' schedules, they know your schedule, they know the bills, they know where everybody goes, they take care of vacations, they run everything in the house, because they care about everything. You a dude. You just know about your job. You don't know nothing. You don't know nothing else. And guess what? I'm happy. I come home and I'm happy.

Before I explain why I vehemently disagree with this, and how bad this is for young men to hear, let me just say: I believe him. I do think he is genuinely happy with such a setup. And, ultimately, it's up to every man to determine for himself the marriage and home situation he has. If you are happy with the home circumstances Harvey outlines above, then go for it.

But I must tell you that I think this is nuts. Women are always encouraged to maintain their individuality after marriage, to retain a "semblance of independence." An even more disturbing trend that is on the rise is women refusing to take their husband's name. Can you imagine a woman telling Ghengis Khan she wanted to keep her maiden name? The feminist women of today are so emboldened by this hyper-feminized culture they have created that they feel comfortable rebelling against thousands of years of culture and tradition.

Boys, let me be 100% clear on something. If a woman isn't proud to take your name, she isn't the one. It's time to drop her at a Starbucks and block her number.

First, to reduce a man's value or role to simply bringing in the money is unhelpful and disrespectful. I think this completely limits the potential of the man, as well as the potential of the family. To say that as a 'dude', you 'don't know nothing' and 'you don't know nothing else' is a complete capitulation to the feminist agenda and ideology that they have sought to make mainstream. These comments from Steve Harvey are in the same family as the sentiments and representations that television and movie entertainment has foisted upon us, where every male in advertisements and sitcoms these days is portrayed as a stupid, helpless, incompetent, and clueless moron. It's not pro-female, it's ridiculously and outrageously anti-male.

Secondly, what Harvey describes, is not, in any way, a traditional alpha male approach to personal life, marriage, or family. The man is not a passenger. He is in the driver's seat of his home, his business, and his golf cart.

Have you no pride? No ego? No testicles? This is exactly how you got backed into that man cave!

Breaking news: contrary to everything you have been told, real men do give a shit. About almost everything. Being a man means working hard, not just at your job, but constantly around the clock, and with even more emphasis and effort on the family and home. It means not sleeping because you're worried about your children. It means shouldering everything. Alphas always care and take an interest, even in things that may not be their natural forte. He is the guardian of the family's reputation and the custodian of its finances. An alpha male is bothered if people he respects, or someone he is trying to close a business deal with comes over and they leave thinking how tacky his home is decorated, or if it's unclean.

If you don't care about the little things, that makes you a simp. A sucker. That's when you really are clueless and idiotic.

Being a father and a husband are the two most important roles a man can have. That means you are on top of *everything* that is going on in your children's lives, your wife's life, and at home. You know exactly what is going on. You don't just hand over the money you earn and let your wife do whatever she wants. Why shouldn't you take an interest in the color of the new curtains, or at the very least be involved in negotiating the best price when buying them? Let's face it, bartering to get the best price is hardly the female's strongest suit typically (I think most women would agree with that). It is not at all peak masculinity to simply work your butt off and then get no say in the home you live in. It's far more masculine to be involved with your wife to make these decisions. A wife who has respect for you will consult you on these things, or factor your tastes into her choices.

And I haven't even gotten to the children part. Is it manly to not care what school your child is going to go to? Is it manly not to know what extracurricular activities such as self-defense, chess, or tennis your children are doing, and when they are doing them?

It's not manly; it's lazy, it's stupid and possibly even cowardly.

You're not a paycheck, or a bank account. You're a man. Your family's burdens are yours. You are not a tyrant, but you are the boss. You do get a say, and you should get a veto. You're the leader. So, start acting like it; you will thank Nick Adams later.

Take an interest in everything, because if you don't your daughter will end up getting a tattoo, your son will end up paying child support from a one-night stand at the age of nineteen, and your wife will be sneaking off to Black Lives Matter rallies with your neighbor.

When you do take an interest, your female partner will respect you more, because by taking an interest, you are showing strength. You are sending a message to her that she might not necessarily get her way, and that you are the authority figure in the home.

Hollywood – Smoke and Mirrors

As we have established, the perception of alpha male today is all over the map. That's why I'm bringing focus through the Nick Adams (Alpha Male) lens.

One of the biggest culprits in the situation we have today is Hollywood. I'll be the first to tell you – all my life, I've been fascinated by Hollywood. I grew up on 80s and 90s movies, sitcoms and shows.

This is why I have been so disappointed by so many of my 'heroes' when I find out what they are really like in their personal life. It's difficult to divorce the actor from the character.

I mean, George Clooney walks, talks and plays the consummate alpha, and yet it wouldn't surprise me in the slightest if it emerged tomorrow that he'd never set foot in a Hooters before in his life.

Why do men – conservative men – who look masculine and love guns and love grilling and drive trucks – feel they need to make that sort of public pronouncement?

I think alpha confidence means you don't have to virtue signal with a Facebook post. If anything, your woman should be posting about YOU! I believe this is a product of the female culture.

Right there, that's a problem. From a guy's standpoint, we should be thinking, "We've got this covered, ladies, don't worry about it, we will tell you what an alpha is." I digress.

It is the desire to conform and fit in. Social media makes it worse. It stems from a lack of confidence on the man's part in themselves.

It's common culture, in the United States, to speak about your wife like that publicly, and so these men think that if they don't do it, they aren't being good husbands or good men. If you don't do it, you automatically look bad. It becomes the price of admission.

"Honey, why didn't you post anything like that on my birthday? You must not love me as much as X,Y or Z..." And then, of course, he'll go and post a nine-page love letter.

It becomes a pissing contest between men on who can be the biggest lover boy on the planet. Where is this energy when it comes time to praise a man? When I made my first hole in one earlier this year, I was overwhelmed with messages of congratulations and support from masculine guys all around the world. No, I'm a happily single guy, so this doesn't apply to me, but I have several friends who got holes-in-one and never heard a peep of congratulations from their wives, let alone a glowing, sappy post on social media. It's imperative for men to become their own cheerleaders.

Here's an alpha action item for you: make a conscious effort today to compliment a man. I don't just mean congratulating him if he hits a great drive, I mean really digging deep and saying something heartfelt. Alpha males should actively sharpen each other's iron on a daily basis. Let your male friends know how they inspire you, how their greatness pushes you to achieve more. A few well-timed words of encouragement between alpha males can spark a whole lot of sharpening!

Another incredible difference between American men and men in other countries that I have observed is the contrast in public and private behaviors.

Beware the fake lions in public that are genuine mice at home.

The men I grew up around were loud and dominant at home, but in public settings were always quiet.

Here in America, men that I know are absolute *mice* at home – that have no say, are barely respected by their wife and kids – are absolute lions in social settings, on social media about sport, politics or a news article. They are super argumentative, loud and dominant in these public forums.

They are the opposite! Loud in public; quiet at home. The home is your domain, that's where your roar should be the loudest!

Why are they argumentative over if X player should have been benched in the third quarter, but don't say a peep when their wife hasn't done the laundry in a week?

The other thing that is so nauseatingly beta here in America, and yet so common (has happened to me often) is when men come up to you when you show up at a social function with an attractive woman and babble – "What is she doing with you?" or "How did you get her?"

It's time we turn the tables. I've made a habit out of approaching women and rizzing up the men they arrived with – "Wow, what's he doing here with you, did he lose a bet?" or "Aren't you a lucky lady getting to walk around on the arm of this masculine hunk of meat?"

You're the catch, not her.

Get some balls, fellas! But back to Hollywood...

The worst gift that Hollywood has given men is what I call the "leading man/superhero complex." It runs so incredibly deep in

American male culture, and it explains why men are dominated by women, as well as so many of the actions of American men.

This is a movie-set mentality where the man behaves like a superhero, where he swoops in, picks up and saves the woman in distress, solving all her problems, and they go on to live happily ever after.

Seek women without makeup, plastic surgery, and tattoos

It's why American men pick fights with other men about women they don't even know. It's why men marry women that are liabilities. It's why men marry women that have already been married, and sometimes more than once. It's why men take on other men's children, even when there is very little gain to them. It's why a man feels that if a wife is unhappy, it is a man's job to fix it. It's why a man will take back a woman who has cheated on him.

American men have a superhero complex. A noble desire to put others above self has served our nation well throughout history, but the radical feminists have weaponized this trait to their benefit. Perhaps the most demonstrative example of this complex was Will Smith's meltdown at the 94th Academy Awards toward Chris Rock in March 2022.

Previous to this moment, I was a big fan of Will Smith. Love all the Bad Boys movies, 'Enemy of the State', 'The Pursuit of Happiness', all of that. So it gives me no pleasure to say what I am about to say, but it must be said.

Will Smith is a pussy.

He laughed at Chris Rock's joke, but then when his wife flashed him a dirty look, he went and hit the guy. That's about as beta a move as there is, being ruled by your wife's feelings

The moment a man is held hostage by what his woman thinks, he has lost his masculinity

That's not noble, alpha, brave, or chivalrous. That's beta virtue-signaling.

But Smith suffered from this leading man or superhero complex, where he felt obligated to take action because American culture suggests that females are a protected species. He felt he was almost in a movie (the irony) where his wife's honor had been injured, and the script required him to initiate a physical altercation. Most men seem to have this 'movie set' mentality.

The truth is in 2022 Jada Pinkett Smith was more than capable of defending herself. Of course, as a result of this beta behavior, Will Smith lost everything.

I don't really like getting into the details of anyone's personal life as it's not my business but from public statements and admissions from Jada Pinkett Smith herself regarding marital infidelity and other things, I must really ask – was she the hill Will Smith really wanted to die on? From a man's perspective (a highly accomplished celebrity male, no less), was she worth defending over something so insignificant?

Women will routinely use their wiles to manipulate a man into action. In Will Smith's case, he was spurred into action by a look on his wife's face.

If you're a true man, you don't get manipulated or influenced. It's not healthy to fear your wife. And you don't bow to pressure.

I was dating a girl in 2022, and about a month in, while having dinner one night, she started railing against Andrew Tate. She'd seen a video clip of him earlier the same afternoon. "He's this; he's that. I can't stand him. Someone needs to put him in his place." I just quietly absorbed it all. Then she said, "Wait...you don't actually like him do you? Oh my God, you totally like him, this is why you're so quiet." I said, "Yes, I'm a big fan of the Top G, and I can particularly relate to his relationship with his father."

She said, "OMG, Nick. This is gonna be a problem. I don't know that I can be with someone that likes Andrew Tate."

Now let me pause the story here.

I want you to know that this girl was a solid nine. Smokin'. Head turnin'. Dead from neck up (if brains were dynamite, I'm not sure she could have blown her nose), but certainly hot to trot.

Without missing a beat, I rhetorically asked her, "You don't think you can be with me if I'm a fan of Andrew Tate? Have a nice evening. Bye." And with that, I pulled out three one hundred dollar bills and left them on the table, and walked out.

Again, the moment a man is held hostage by what his woman thinks, he has lost his masculinity. If you must change or suppress your view or opinion on something because it makes your woman mad or you fear her reaction, you're a beta.

I'm very popular on Cameo with young men, and I often get requests for advice.

Quite a few times, a group of buddies have requested a Cameo from me for one of their friends that roasts their friend because they say that he no longer supports Donald Trump publicly because his wife won't let him.

I've also had a few requests for advice from young men going out on dates with ladies that don't like Donald Trump. *I know she doesn't like Trump, Nick, and I love him, but I really want to get in her pants, she's so hot, so should I pretend and go along and act like I don't like him either?*

Hell no.

Having made these mistakes in my own early years, with other things, long before Donald Trump was President, I am very passionate about this. This is not a time for diplomacy.

This is a time to stand up for yourself, which leads me to one of my most important rules.

Chapter 9
Relationship Advice

If from the very first date, you are ameliorating your positions, opinions, or worldview from the person you are sitting opposite, you are in for a world of hurt.

Look, if you do it at any time, you are asking for trouble – but to do it from the very start, you're in for disaster.

In a relationship, put down your foot early

From the very beginning, you need to be honest, straightforward and show that you are your own man. In fact, if anything, if you deem the difference in opinion significant enough, you should be seeking to change her opinion, not have her change yours. An alpha leader creates his own consensus, he doesn't conform to it.

Jedediah Bila has a great podcast, and back in November 2022, she made comments that I considered so spot on, so incredibly on the mark. Not only that, but I've also actually never heard another commentator anywhere with any kind of platform make such observations. This is why I'm a big fan of hers.

This is what she said:

"What I see that really disturbs me in society a lot are these guys... Sometimes they look really masculine, right? They're tall. They're built. They give the illusion of this guy in control.

They walk into their own homes and they walk on eggshells 24 hours a day, seven days a week, out of fear they're going to upset the Queen, and the Queen is going to take it out on her subject. Meaning him. So, they're just doing whatever makes her happy to the point where they have no authority whatsoever about not anything, even their own day, you know.

They're afraid to upset her with this or that, and you know those households... you know where the guy walks on eggshells and he says one thing wrong, she darts a look at him... like, looks like daggers just coming out of her eyes... He quickly shuts up, and he just hopes and prays that she will have forgotten it by the time dinner is done."

Amen, sister!

These remarks showcase that she understands the false definition of alpha male and masculinity in America and provide the basis for the overwhelmingly majority of Nick's Commandments.

What she describes here, tens of millions of men are living right now. And they think that it's normal. That it's just the price of being with a woman, married or unmarried. That's just the way women are. They're sensitive, and when a man is a man, he unavoidably irritates the woman. It sucks, but it is what it is. Have to live with it. If you don't want to be lonely in life, you just have to suck it up.

No! No, you don't have to live with it. You don't have to be miserable. I don't care what women say, it's not normal to be a grown ass man and be scared of your wife. You respect her, but you never tiptoe on eggshells in your own home. You do not have to tolerate that emotional and mental abuse from her. Only betas do it. An alpha king will not put up with it.

An alpha king will put his foot down early, and establish the ground rules. That's not controlling, that's not tyrannical, that's not being a bully – that's being a male leader knowing what a female is like. An alpha is always in control of his life. If your home situation is like what Jedidah describes, you don't control your life. It's pretty simple.

Men, you need breaks from women. Women, you need breaks from men. It's no different than parents needing a break from their children once in a while. You need space to speak and act as you please, to not prioritize your female partner, and to not define yourself in relation to your duties, but to express who you were before you committed to them. Men who never get this lose their edge, and they end up living this hellish life that they can't escape where they are punished for saying something their wife doesn't like.

There are social media videos of a groups of men – you have seen them – a man gets a call from his wife, or has a missed call from his wife and before he rings her – and his three or four friends get off their motorbikes, or get off their golf carts and pull out a drill and make noises – playing along to make sure he doesn't draw his wife's ire.

"When you have a missed call from your wife, and she thinks you're helping friends build a deck" is the title of another viral video.

This is not alpha behavior. It has become normalized standard American male behavior that makes you chuckle, but it is not normal, and it certainly isn't masculine.

Over the last couple of years, I have fielded countless questions from men in relationships. I want there to be some instruction and suggested action in this book, not just a series of warnings. So, let's go through them.

What do you do if she tells you she is hangry and wants to go out to eat?

When your partner tells you she is hungry/hangry and she wants to get food, you tell her very calmly, but forcefully that we aren't going anywhere, eat what's in the fridge. We just had (insert x) yesterday, finish that.

If she wishes to debate the matter, repeat: "We aren't going anywhere because all that's going to happen if we go somewhere is you're going to get into a worse mood, which is going to get me into a bad mood, and you will probably slam the car door, or raise your voice or make a comment about my family, and things will escalate. Meanwhile, there's lots of food in the fridge!

What to do if she raises her voice?

Stay calm and stay in control. Tell her that its unacceptable behavior, and even though you have a much bigger voice box and could be louder than her if you wanted, you won't be competing her. Explain to her that if she does it again, she can start packing her bags and stay with her mother.

This is an opportune time to introduce another one of my Commandments: **Display emotional control, and never show vulnerability or weakness, and never apologize.**

What to do when she is rude to your family or friends?

If she is rude to your family or close friends, this must be immediately addressed. It is unacceptable, and again as she is in a leadership position with the children, they are likely to think that such behavior is fine. She sets the tone. If it is met with any resistance, or happens again, start packing her bags for her.

Family is a political ideology

Now, some of you may be reading this, and thinking this is just too much. This all doesn't matter that much. Wrong! It matters more than you could ever possibly realize.

Let me explain to you in terms you might better understand. The concept of "family" must be treated as though it is a political ideology. What do I mean by that?

If she can be rude to your family or your friend, she can come home tomorrow and say: "My friend is becoming a man, and I'm really happy about it, and we are going to stay best friends, and I think we should get him to baptize our children..."

If there is a set of values that a family is going to live by, they must stick to those values, including the woman. If you don't enforce those values, and it is your job as the man to be the enforcer, then you are going to be stuck with someone who has no values, stuck with a rudderless family, and children that are going to be on puberty blockers and all sorts of crap, all because you had no control.

The control must start with "you're not getting the food you want - eat what's at home," "you're not buying that - stick with what you've got." Because if you don't control it, it ends with your kids getting out of control doing drugs and becoming part of the woke mob at college. That's what happens when there is no uniformity, no consistency of thought.

It's not easy. There is suffering and pain and struggle, as outlined in an earlier discussion surrounding happiness and alphas. Sometimes it's hard to be around your partner's family, but it's worth doing. The same way that being a conservative is not easy. You lose jobs, you miss opportunities, you shed friends, and if you wear a red cap in the wrong city, you'll get spat at. But it's worth it.

Discipline

I believe that every single problem in America today can be traced back to the absence of strength that can only come from masculinity:

- Discipline in schools
- Gender dysphoria
- Political correctness/wokeness
- Disrespect for police
- Participation trophies
- Safe spaces

But if there was one thing that I would say pre-dates or is the basis for the loss of masculinity, that is the true origin of all our problems, its discipline in the home.

Here's the cold hard truth: it's all nurture and no discipline. Parenting has collapsed. Women are at the head of most households, and as a result most children have no discipline.

More than 25 million children in the U.S. don't live with a biological father. Studies show again and again – children that grow up without a father are more likely to live in poverty, commit crime, and go to jail.

Modern woke feminism is a destructive movement. It has decimated the family, eliminated unity, and villainized fifty percent of the population.

Children are medicated and pawned off and grow up with no structure because the men in the household, if there is one at all, are second fiddle to the women. It is an enormous indictment on our society that we put our children on heavy medications because parents don't want to deal with their boys being boys.

When you go outside of your home, you are not only representing yourself, but you're also taking the name of your mother and father with you.

The moment they leave the front porch and set foot on the sidewalk; your child represents you. Just like you represent your mother and father. It might sound old-fashioned; it may sound counter to American individualism, but it is the philosophy with the most potential to ensure decency and honor in your child.

Just like a woman, your child responds to strength. Sometimes you should say 'no' to your child just for the sake of it. It's healthy.

You are their parent, not their friend. Act like it.

Treat your children like adults, from the age of five

You should be speaking in full sentences to your children, as though they were adults, from an early age. You should be correcting their speech, and rectifying incorrect voice inflection or bad verbal tics regularly. You should also begin dressing them, not all the time, but occasionally in "adult clothes." You should be waking them up early, and getting them into a routine. You set their rules, not them. No iPads or electronics of any kind at the dinner table, and no televisions in bedrooms. Again, anything short of this is just lazy parenting.

They will have freedom, but there will be boundaries. You can encourage your children to be part of a spirited discussion, but if they are factually incorrect and get exposed in that exchange, you tell them to stop, and send them to their room to 'lick their wounds' to be better prepared next time.

When I was a child, and I spoke too much at the dinner table when we had guests over, my paternal grandfather would tell me that "children are to be seen, not heard." My maternal grandfather would say to me "Silence is gold; speaking is silver." I know that may not be the mainstream American view these days for raising children, but there is a lot of value to it. I know the situations when it is not going to be good for me to talk. I can think of a few women I have dated, and a few friends I've had that I wish had learned the same things because they didn't know when it was time to shut up and paid the price. That's what happens when there is an absence of discipline.

Perfecting your child is going to be a struggle. There will be pain and suffering, but you can't become a Navy Seal without going through Hell Week, and yet that seems to be the approach of so many parents today.

My father outright refused to engage in any baby talk with me. When I was five years old, he began to treat me like an adult. He didn't dumb things down for me, he didn't cut me any slack, he didn't accept if I mispronounced a word or made a grammatical error, he held me to account. In many ways, I credit my generational oratorical talent to this upbringing. If you want your child to behave a certain way, it's up to you, as the man of the house, to set the tone. This includes the relationship with your partner when it comes to discipline. The most common thing I see and hear about are wives stopping or persuading their husbands out of disciplining their children. Bottom line: don't let your wife talk you out of or stop you from disciplining your child.

You want your children to be resilient and tough. If the temperature is too warm at home, your child will be a snowflake outside. Our culture today is worried about 'micro-aggressions' and this is producing weaker and less-resilient citizens.

This is again of particular note to your sons, to the boys of America. The culture is currently creating victims, not heroes. Alphas are not victims (even though we are victimized and have every right to complain). If left to our sick culture, our boys will turn out the opposite of alpha.

Teach your boys to be men before the world teaches them to be women.

As I have written this book, I have realized that discipline truly underpins every one of my commandments.

You need discipline to walk away from sex. If you are going to know more about your tax bracket than your tattoos, you have to be disciplined. You've got to be disciplined to sit down and read boring stuff. You must exercise discipline in telling your wife how to be with your family. You have to be disciplined to call out car door slamming.

Parental discipline is the first action to influence masculinity in the culture. The weakness or absence of it means masculinity wanes. To be an alpha male, you typically have to be raised with discipline and have discipline. It's a big factor that ties into everything.

These days, most American men have never had discipline their whole life, with the important exception of one area: work. That's because the government doesn't give you anything. In Australia and Europe, it's the opposite. *The only thing people in those countries don't have discipline in is work.*

Discipline was one of the biggest things I grew up with and around, and I know most of my American friends missed out.

The good news is that you can teach discipline to someone that has never had it. You can build a routine, use the goldmine in between that is your mind, and read affirmations every day out loud in front of the mirror (at the end of the book, you will have a comprehensive list).

Chapter 10
Boys Will Be Boys

Modern woke feminism, and the nasty women and pathetic men that represent it, have spent the last few decades trying to clip the wings of every young alpha eagle almost from the moment he is born.

Their justification? Men have all the power, privilege, and rights. Masculinity is the issue, and men are the problem. They just need to stop thrusting. The patriarchy has been keeping women down since the beginning of time, and it is time for revenge. All men to the back. Young men must atone for the sins of generations past.

See why I call them nasty? And don't get me started on their steak-deprived, vegan-tapas-eating beta counterparts with their little pink spoons. These feminist broads just don't get it.

Cupcake, I'm not intimidating; you're intimidated. There is a difference. I'm not mean, and I'm not aggressive. I'm honest and assertive, and that makes you uncomfortable.

More than that, babycakes, it's not me that makes you uncomfortable. It's my presence that challenges your comfort. Now, here's where the bad news gets really bad: Nick Adams (Alpha Male) will not be less of a man just so you can feel better about yourself.

And we will manspread our wings and reach full flight despite you doing everything to thwart God's great plans for alphas.

Muffing Masculinity

When I was growing up, I was in trouble a fair bit. Whenever I was called into the principal's office, I heard the words 'I know boys will be boys', I knew I was home free. I knew the punishment couldn't be too dire. Of course, in the late nineties and early 2000s, being a normal boy wasn't yet the serious liability it is today in a classroom. In 2023, I would definitely have been expelled!

"Boys will be boys" has always been a phrase that emphasizes that people should not be surprised when boys or men act in a rough or rowdy way because this is part of the male character. It's true. Boys need to blow off steam and can get aggressive. It's a natural and biological impulse. In today's schooling, what was once considered standard 'boy behavior' is now considered 'problematic' behavior, worthy of expulsion.

Boys are being told to sit back and let the women take the lead. They are being guilted from a young age for being a male and told masculinity is a bad thing. *"Girl's behavior is the gold standard in schools. Boys are treated like defective girls,"* observes psychologist Michael Thompson. The Left is happy to have thirty-seven genders as long as "male" isn't one of them.

It's the mission of the Left to repress alpha males from the early onset of kindergarten, or even Pre-K. You must ask yourself. Why is the Left fighting so hard to make government-funded Pre-K a reality? The answer is simple. To put the state in control of the children as early as possible. To make men weak and effeminate from an early age. They seek to give boys less time at home, and more time with the woke school administrators. Less time to watch Tim Tebow highlights on YouTube with your father and more time surrounded by soy-latte-sipping educators.

In the tenth grade, I had this teacher, Mr. Dixon, who kept picking on me, even outside the classroom. One day, at the end of the seventh period, I went up to him and told him – "Mr. Dixon, you don't like me, and I don't like you. So, it would be in both of our best interests if you stayed away from me." Boom! That's how an alpha solves the problem. Mr. Dixon never crossed me again, because even at my young age, I knew I could assert my masculinity and create change. I made it clear I wouldn't just take it lying down. Of course, in 2023, I would likely have had the police called on me and been prescribed Ritalin.

Then there is the actual curriculum. The male imagination is very different to the female imagination. Just as girls respond and engage with certain books and movies, boys respond and engage with different materials. There's only one problem. Today's education curriculum and total system doesn't cater to boys or the male imagination at all – it all centered around female learning. And then when boys get restless or inattentive or a bit noisy, we come down on them like a ton of bricks. The patience and understanding so emphasized by these woke education types go straight out the door.

The feminist dogma of the education system is responsible for this feminizing and targeting of American boys that has left them languishing academically but American girls thriving. Not only that, young men are dropping out of high school at record highs.

In case the Democrats skipped the class on geopolitics in favor of the Land Rights for Bisexual Indigenous Whales class, let me educate them. When the Chinese and all these other people come for us, we need 100% of the population thriving, not 50%. There are very destructive long-term consequences in telling the male half of the population to curtail their ambitions, to watch their 'toxic masculinity', and to shelve their dreams. Picture this: the survival of your country is at stake. Do you want a rifle to be placed in the small, soft hands of a nonbinary, gender studies major, who advertises they/them pronouns? Or do you want someone like George Patton? I'm taking Patton every time.

If you can believe it – the PC junkies now insist that the age-old saying - "boys will be boys" - uttered by parents and teachers alike for millennia, is a dangerous phrase and are actively discouraging its use. Most prominent among these fruit loops, ironically, is the Left-wing psychology community and, of course, the LGBTQIAWTF+ pronoun brigade.

It reminds me of that time at college when I was with a buddy who was only an alpha male in training at the time. He was a good bloke, but he didn't have the Nick Adams (Alpha Male) confidence. We were at the bar pounding a couple of ice-cold domestics when one festively plump lesbian with a Camp Lejeune haircut and another rather pretty lipstick lesbian recognized us as the conservatives on campus.

The sheila with the high and tight, we'll call her Barb, immediately began berating my friend. He had asked a question at a political event earlier that day that she hadn't appreciated. Our mere presence had enraged her to the point that she could not control her lesbian fury. I'll note that she was quite well-built for a woman, but her behavior made me think the campus rumors about her steroid use might have had some truth to them. Now, it takes a lot for me to unwrap my teeth from a few brews, but the unprovoked attack on my genius buddy and the opportunity to correct a sheila behaving like a man will do it every time.

70

Taking a long, deep sip of my beer, and with a light smack of my lips, I said, "Excuse me, muffin, but my friend can ask whatever he wants – he's a bloke. We all have a bit of cheek in us. Boys will be boys. And we are doing what boys do. We're having a beer, so just piss off."

Her pretty friend looked at me in awe, unsure of whether to throw a punch or throw herself into my lap. She stammered, but after a nudge from her manly companion, she snapped back. "That's bullshit," Barb shouted. "You're a dick."

I took another sip and said, "Well, now, you're hardly an authority on the matter, are you, love? If the wand doesn't have a couple of engines underneath it, it's not a real wand."

If looks could kill, I would have been a dead man. She let out a huge, flustered sigh, a mixture of exasperation, disgust, and anger, at a decibel level even a whale would have been proud of. She turned to her lipstick lesbian friend and said "Let's go, baby." Her friend, whose glazed over eyes were still on me, didn't even look in her direction as she rather ashamedly said, "Uh, I, uh think I'm going to stay here a little longer."

Barb glanced at her with a look of disbelief. "Oh my God, this is unbelievable!" she cried out. She stormed out, her pounding strides shaking the floor with every step.

I smiled, my award-winning dimple more pronounced than ever before, as her friend slid onto the chair next to me and my mate.

"Hi, I'm April," she said. "Nice to meet you, Ape," I replied. "This is going to be new and different for me," she said. I took one last sip of my domestic and turned to her with a twinkle in my eye, "No worries, Ape, I'll show you the ropes."

That night I made an honest woman out of April, and men all over the world should thank me. Boys will be boys!

College

Since we are on the subject of colleges, let me tell you - it's not just grade school and high school that no longer cater to alpha males, but also colleges. Not only are male students graduating from high school at historically low levels, but colleges now give preference to women, LGBTQ, and minority applicants. As a result, you are seeing fewer and fewer alpha males pursuing education in college. It is tragic, it is grossly unfair, and it is the result of the overpowering female influence in higher education. Who wants to pay $20,000 per year to hear some over-soyed, noodle-armed, gender-dysphoric, tweed-jacketed imbecile professor wail on about structural white-hetero-patriarchal historical abuses?

Why participate in academically sanctioned shaming of men? Why operate in an anti-male environment? By the time an alpha male sets foot on his college campus, the assault on his manhood is already well underway. Not only will he be criticized for the actions of his ancestors, he will also be held accountable for the actions of men who died hundreds of years ago and thousands of miles away. He will be otherized, to borrow a leftist term, simply for being born a male.

Then there are college graduation rates. Men have a much lower likelihood of actually finishing college. Why? The education system and its rulers have made it clear that they consider the male identity to be at odds with higher education. Colleges are inhospitable to real men. The anti-maleness is rampant. They cater to everyone except regular, everyday men. They make regular alpha males feel uncomfortable and unable to speak or act freely, so men simply abandon college campuses. Every man is essentially welcomed to college by being implicated as a potential rapist. Fraternities are hated and scrutinized, like the media scrutinizes Donald Trump, whereas bad behavior at a sorority gets the Hunter Biden treatment.

While women are welcomed with abundant single-sex spaces and organizations, men are sent to the back of the bus. Nearly every western university offers feminist gender studies majors, I can't think of any that offer a male studies program. If they had, I'd have graduated as a double major and possibly be teaching the classes, that much is certain.

Feminists run colleges, and gutless male administrators bend over and take it. It's not about equality; it's about "equity," or more accurately, revenge. More than that, anti-maleness is structural, embedded, and endemic. Young men are immediately assumed to be behaving badly, or about to behave badly and in need of re-programming.

I know all about it from personal experience.

When I was doing my postgraduate degree in education at the University of Sydney, I had two brief high school teacher internships that were compulsory. The schools were 'randomly' selected and then assigned to you. My first school was a selective, highly academic, all-boys school which was great. But, as luck would have it, for my second internship, I drew a school that would require two trains and a bus to get there, meaning it would be a two hour plus round trip.

In true alpha male fashion, I decided to take matters into my own hands. That afternoon I walked up to the private girls school just a five-minute walk from where I lived and entered the main reception area. Within minutes, I had the two female receptionists laughing, putty in my hands, eager to potentially house their shoes under my bed for a few hours. Before I knew it, I had successfully sold them the idea of doing my internship at the school, and they even assigned me to a teacher.

You little beauty, I thought. Mission accomplished. Now, I'll go and let the lady in charge of the internships in the Education Department know that I went and organized it myself, as the other school was too far away, and I saved myself ten hours in travel for the week. I went and gently knocked on the professor's door, and as soon as I eased my way slowly in and saw her, I knew World War III would soon start. The first tell was the rainbow flag sticker, closely followed by the Ellen DeGeneres dancing YouTube video, that had been paused on her desktop computer, and finished off with two stickers – Kevin 07 (the campaign sticker of the socialist Australian PM at the time) and something else referencing the national Australian apology to the Aborigines.

I politely explained the situation and updated her on the private girls school internship.

"You went and organized your own?" she incredulously repeated.

I resisted the urge to respond, "Lady, are your ears painted on or what? I'm standing less than three feet from you. An alpha male is speaking, listen and learn!" "Yes, ma'am, I did." I said, mustering as much cockiness as possible, grinning like a Cheshire cat, my left dimple showing all its glory while the eye twinkled charismatically. *"And I'm not going to apologize for it."* That did it. She exploded.

"That was completely inappropriate and against the rules. You must accept the school you are assigned; it is not a choice. You already did an internship at a school similar in nature to the all-private girls school, and we will insist on a variety of experiences. Frankly, I am appalled at your audacity to simply approach another school," she said, huffing and puffing between sentences. "It is completely unprofessional and unfit for someone who wishes to become a teacher. What that high school must now think of our university."

I won't lie, I was offended by her outburst, but I decided to take the high road. "Ma'am, there is no need to raise your voice. I can hear you perfectly well. I don't really care what kind of experience you would like me to have, ideally," I said, looking her straight in the eye. "This is my education, my life, and it makes absolutely no sense to add ten hours to my week just because of your idea of variety. This is a school just like any other, I took the initiative (something teachers need to do) and organized everything. If anything, you should be thanking me."

She sat there, mouth agape, her brain desperately trying to compute the overload of masculinity coming from this dapper 23-year-old. I could tell she was struggling to process her emotions. After her buffering ended, she screamed: "Who do you think you are? How dare you speak to me in this way? You will NOT throw your weight around here, nor will you intimidate me as a woman."

Very calmly, I responded, "That is a generous description of yourself, ma'am. Based on your manner in this brief interaction, it's pretty clear you are nothing more than an inflexible lefty feminist bureaucrat on a power trip. I have done nothing to intimidate you other than to be confident. You just can't handle my masculinity."

At this point, she lost it. The tension in the room was so thick you could have cut it with a knife. "You will leave right now, or I am going to call security!"

With my work complete, I flashed her another award-winning Nick Adams (Alpha Male) smile, turned heel, and left slowly, buttoning my middle blue blazer gold button. As I was closing the door behind me, I popped my head back in quickly and cheekily quipped, "You're welcome to continue watching Ellen now."

Chapter 11
The Feminization of Sport

Few things get me more excited than heading to Hooters to meet up with some masculine guys and pound a few domestic beers while watching football. Sports are something that has brought men together for generations. Sports transcend age, race, class, religion, and partisan affiliation.

Watching five different sports on twenty different televisions all at once with a group of guys, now THAT'S American exceptionalism right there! No country in the world does sports like we do here in the U.S.

I love cricket, rugby union, and rugby league, but I don't get to watch them very much anymore having lived in America for so long. Instead, my days are filled with the NFL, college football, baseball, basketball, and ice hockey (whenever I can catch it). I'm a tennis fan, too. Novak "NoVax" Djokovic is my favorite male athlete and one of the biggest alphas to have ever traversed this planet. He's been called the Tim Tebow of tennis, and I don't believe it's an exaggeration. And pretty much every women's beach volleyball player is my favorite female athlete!

I remember once getting into a cab in Texas, on my way to AT&T Stadium in Arlington to watch the Cowboys play and the driver asked me if I liked the Dallas Cowboys.

"Sure, I like the Dallas Cowboys," I said. "but if I'm being honest with you, I much prefer the Dallas Cowboys Cheerleaders." He began to laugh hysterically, struggling to keep the vehicle in the lane.

Wokeness has flooded sports

But on a serious note, it's been incredibly disturbing to watch how sports in all countries have gone woke. To me, it's one of the greatest examples of the deep state's all-out assault on alpha males and our way of life. A prime example of this would be the NFL's disgusting infatuation with the repulsive Taylor Swift/Travis Kelce relationship. Men tune in to watch football, not shots of Taylor Swift doing special celebration handshakes with dangerous criminal and sexual deviant Jackson Mahomes. The Kelce/Swift relationship is so deeply upsetting that it could be worthy of its own standalone book. Why can't these people just let us men watch a football game in peace? It's not just bad television, it's detrimental to men's mental health. Seeing one of our former brothers in alphadom, Travis Kelce, continue to be emasculated on national television by his pro-Hamas girlfriend was a harrowing experience for all alpha males throughout the first half of the 2023 season. His betrayal will be dealt with at a later time. That is just one instance that fits into a far greater trend.

Alpha male sports heroes like Urban Meyer, Tim Tebow, and America First patriot Nick Bosa are consistently slandered in the sports media for their faith in God and strong traditional values. It wouldn't be so concerning if it weren't so effective. I recall a trip to the bakery last year to pick up some fresh sourdough bread. While I was in line, I overheard an effeminate slender bloke with a wiry mustache and his male companion discussing Netflix's "Swamp Kings" docuseries – the only thing on Netflix worth watching – about Urban Meyer and Tim Tebow's tenure at the University of Florida.

The mustached fellow said he stopped watching when Tim Tebow appeared because he "couldn't take him seriously." I was gobsmacked by the comment but composed myself and leaned in. "Career completion percentage under 50? What a joke!" The effeminate male companion interjected, "Did he even average seven air yards per attempt in the NFL?" "I highly doubt it," the mustached man replied. At this point, I had heard enough. I stepped forward confidently and put a finger in each of their chests.

"Listen here. You don't know the ball." I said. "In Tim Tebow's only year as an NFL starter, he led Denver to the playoffs with a 7-4 record. He had a 2-1 TD/INT ratio and averaged over 5.5 yards per carry on the ground. Frankly, I consider his playoff win over alpha male Ben Roethlisberger to be a Super Bowl-level achievement," I said with mounting intensity. "Get Tim Tebow's name OUT of your nasty mouth!"

The two men were shaking in their Doc Martens boots, clearly intimidated by my masculinity. All they could utter was a quiet acknowledgment of the validity of my statistics as they scurried away to find bread and pastries elsewhere.

I took a deep breath and stepped forward to the counter to be greeted by my baker, Georgios, with a warm, masculine embrace. He walked back to fetch my usual daily order, two loaves of sourdough bread, so fresh that they're hot to the touch.

While waiting, I noticed an alluring Cuban figure wearing a #85 teal Jacksonville Jaguars Tim Tebow jersey approaching me.

"I couldn't help but overhear...That was really brave of you to stand up for Coach Meyer and Tim Tebow like that," she said. "I shouldn't be surprised," I replied. "All it took was one glance to realize they didn't know football."

Let the boys play

When I grew up, there could be a melee on the field with dozens of punches thrown, and next to no punishment. Now, players face suspensions and financial penalties. The only sport that remains masculine is ice hockey. They still let fights and scraps happen. A must-watch for every alpha male is the 1985 classic – 'Youngblood' – starring Rob Lowe and Patrick Swayze.

Professional sports USED to be a place for alpha males to thrive under a pure meritocracy. However, over recent years, there has been a pervasive attack to dismantle that culture of accomplishment and pollute it with woke political ideologies. No greater example of the breakdown of the meritocracy of sports than the NFL's blackballing of Tim Tebow.

Anyone with half a brain that follows the NFL can see there are a LOT of terrible quarterbacks in the league. Ryan Tannehill, Jalen Hurts, Baker Mayfield, Kenny Pickett, and Joe Burrow just to name a few. There are not now, nor have there ever been, 32 better quarterbacks in the league than Tim Tebow. There just aren't.

Let me state the obvious again: Tim Tebow's exit from the NFL had nothing to do with his on-field performance. He was forced out of the league because of his outspoken faith in Jesus Christ as his Lord and Savior. Political correctness and the corrupt NFL won, and the fans lost.

My sources tell me Tebow had done "more than enough" to make the Jaguars 2021 roster, albeit as a tight end. Head coach Urban Meyer had carved out the perfect role for Tebow in his offense as a field-stretching vertical threat tight end but had the move vetoed by higher-ups in the league office. My sources also told me that was a wake-up call for Coach Meyer. He wasn't in college anymore, and he couldn't build the roster he needed to succeed. A few months later, he would find himself driven out of the league for similar reasons. The NFL is not a welcoming environment for alpha males in 2024.

Female referees and coaches are another great example of this. Almost every major sport has been placing an emphasis on hiring female referees and coaches despite a woman's inability to compete in athletics to the highest level like men. It's a biological fact that men are stronger, bigger, and faster than women, yet it's now required that we all pretend biology does not exist and that men's sports should be refereed and coached by inferior female athletes.

Robin DeLorenzo is a female referee in the NFL, and she's been consistently rated as one of the worst refs in the game. In an NFL.com piece titled 'Next Woman Up,' DeLorenzo said, "I had many jobs. I was a teacher's assistant, ran background checks and fingerprints for TSA PreCheck, was a bartender and so many other things. I eventually chose football over everything else."

I think that says it all right there. Robin DeLorenzo was fingerprinting airline passengers before the NFL came calling to meet a diversity quota. The woke NFL is compromising the integrity of its product for an affirmative action hire *and bragging about it.* But it does not end there.

Forcing women's sports down our throat

I know I'm not the only one who has noticed the concerted effort to force women's sports on the men of America lately. A few months back, I headed off to the gym to pump some iron after my breakfast of 6 eggs, black coffee, and a rare 39 oz porterhouse.

When I strutted into the gym, I immediately noticed they had every single TV playing ESPN's SportsCenter.

Normally, I would consider this a good thing. I like to have something masculine, like sports highlights, playing in the background while I'm on the leg press. Unfortunately, ESPN has become so woke that SportsCenter's programming has suffered as a result. The entire time I was pumping iron and thrusting hard, woke ESPN only covered women's sports. From women's fighting to the WNBA — it's like masculinity means nothing to these people.

Now, I will concede one thing about the WNBA. Some of their players, while not very good at basketball, are more masculine than many NBA players today. Who's more of a man, Britney Griner or LeBron James? The jury is still out on that one. Regardless of where you land on that question, pretty much everybody agrees that neither one of them could hold a candle to the alpha male basketball stars of the past, like Larry Bird, Mark Price, or John Stockton.

Women invading men's sports

The unscientific Left's latest crusade is to pressure male leagues to accept female participants.

The most public, egregious, and ridiculous example of this was when female advocates claimed females should be kickers in the NFL and NCAA football. For weeks, the entire sports universe was forced to hear about Sarah Fuller, a female soccer player, who kicked off for the Vanderbilt football team. She was the first female to play in a men's football game. The kick was an absolute disaster, barely going 20 yards in the air and almost veering out of bounds.

In addition to female coaching, refereeing, and playing, there is also a concerted effort to push females as sports analysts and commentators, despite the fact that they never actually played the sport they're analyzing. Even in Australia, which as previously noted, has retained more of its masculinity than many other Western nations, all the footy shows and football commentators that were 100% male for the first 30 years of my life, now heavily feature female hosts.

Look no further than the recent example of Jeff Garcia and Mina Kimes going at it over Jimmy Garoppolo. Garcia was a pro-bowl level quarterback in the NFL and took exception to criticism that Kimes was making on Jimmy G, and pointed out how Kimes has never actually played quarterback in the NFL (let alone assumed any position...on a field that is) before, so he (Garcia) might have more knowledge on the situation. The media and liberal apparatus pounced on Garcia immediately calling him every name under the sun and pushing for him to be canceled from the sports world for his 'misogyny.'

They can't be satisfied with trying to make us watch women's sports either. No, they have to force-feed us female commentators while we're watching men's sports, too. Now, there is nothing wrong with female sports commentators, who are commentating on sports they actually played – tennis, volleyball, golf, beach volleyball, bowling, softball, or women's soccer - but should they really be NFL football analysts when there are people available who actually played the sport?

In 2023, ESPN announced they were extending the contract of Kimes, their "star NFL analyst." **I have forgotten more about football than Kimes will ever know.** She has never played a down of football in her life, yet she will be paid $1.7 million a year to talk about it on TV. Sports media is no longer about sports, it's a DEI program.

But it's not just men who are fed up with this. The day after that contract was announced, I was having a pump at the gym when I couldn't help but overhear two millennial women with tattoos on the StairMaster discussing Mina Kimes.

"If I had known they paid women $1.7 million per year to talk about a sport they've never played, I would have gone into sports media!" the blonde woman said. "I find female voices on football broadcasts very distracting," the brunette said as she nodded in agreement.

She went on to say that she wished ESPN would just focus on the game instead of wokeness, and the blonde hinted that she might not be tuning into Monday Night Football as a result of Kimes' contract.

They both agreed they'd like to see more masculine on-air talents at ESPN and suggested Brett Favre as a suitable upgrade over Kimes. You know you've gone too far when you even lose the tattooed millennial women.

Not only are women now demanding access to men's sports in media, coaching, refereeing, and PLAYIN, but they are also now demanding equal pay in women's leagues compared to men's leagues. **Yes, you read that correctly. WNBA players want to be paid the same as NBA players.**

Even though WNBA teams operate at a net loss, and NBA teams make MILLIONS in profit every year and are worth BILLIONS, they think they deserve more. The worst part is the left-wing media continues to peddle the lie that female athletes are equal to male athletes. That is not true on the field or in the marketplace. If I went to a WNBA game, I'd fall asleep before the first whistle! We've all seen the viral videos where someone offers a stranger the choice between $1 or courtside WNBA tickets. Virtually everyone, male or female, chooses the $1.

There has been a massive push in recent years for the female US soccer team to receive the same pay as the men's US soccer team. On the surface, it doesn't sound so outlandish given the USWNT's success on the field (not counting the 2023 World Cup, where Megan Rapinoe, in a glorious stroke of coincidental irony, missed the penalty kick to leave the United States short of even qualifying for the semi-finals.) I'll get to the economics of it in a second, but let's focus on the pure merit of the argument.

The sheilas think they can hang with the blokes and want to get paid accordingly. I get it. The glaring issue is that they *can't hang with the blokes.* They can't even hang with the high school blokes. In 2016, the USWNT played a friendly match against an under-15 boys team from Dallas. They lost 5-2. That's right, the US Women's National Soccer Team, one of the best female squads in the entire world, got boat-raced by a team of 13 and 14-year-old boys.

It would be easy to dismiss that as a fluke, but it's not just American women who can't seem to keep up with high school boys. That same year, the Australian Women's Soccer Team got blown out, 7-0, by another under-15 boys squad from the UK. There's a long and storied track of this happening. Men and women play sports separately for a reason and there's nothing wrong with that. That's how it should be. That's what's fair!

Now, back to economics. This "equal pay" push ignored all the basic economic facts surrounding the World Cup and soccer – the vast majority of the money was in men's sports, so despite the US Men's team's poor performance, it still generated more revenue for soccer than the US Women's team and their historic 2019 run. The Left wants to ignore the economics of sports all for the sake of pushing woke agendas. They don't live in reality.

It reminds me of the time I was playing doubles tennis (also known as a foursome, coincidentally) at my country club, and a crowd had formed outside the court.

It was a hot day, and the competition was intense. The sweat on our brows glistened in the sunlight. As I chugged my ice-cold La Croix on the change of ends, I caught a group of sheilas decked out like they were going to Wimbledon. They were watching, pointing, and giggling in my general direction. I motioned to the boys that I was putting the game on pause, and moseyed over to the gaggle of geese. "G'day ladies, looking fine today – you actually here to play tennis or just here to admire our alpha physiques?" I inquired, with my famous eye twinkle, and a little curl of the lips.

More giggles. "Actually, one said to me, playfully, "We were going to ask if you would agree to play one set against Marci, because we think she'd beat you. She played tennis in college."

Without hesitation, I said, "Not sure what you are on this morning, sweetheart, but whatever it is, I'd love to be on it!" Then I lowered my voice. "Your tennis analysis must be woeful - she won't even get a game off me." Marci stepped forward. "Well, let's play then," she said, daringly. "Not so fast, darling. What's in it for me?" I responded, not phased in the slightest bit.

The birds all looked at each other quizzically. "What do you mean, what's in it for you?," came the cacophony of voices, practically in unison. I stroked my chin gently in prayerful consideration as the boys had come over to see what the fuss was all about. "I tell you what, Marce, I'll make you a deal. If I win, you must be my ball-girl for the next five games here."

After barely any consideration, and without even asking for something in reciprocity should she win (sheilas have a lot to learn about negotiation), she agreed to it. She had a cocky demeanor about her. I could tell this was a girl who had been told that she could do anything a man could do, only better, for her entire life.

Now, Marci was pretty easy on the eyes, so I knew I could win on the court and off the court.

Even though it was against club rules, I took off my shirt to play, exposing my thick, toned, and tanned arms and barrel chest. I huddled up with the boys while she did some light stretching. We got in close, and Mario, my butcher and dear friend, delivered a rousing pre-game speech. By the time we broke our huddle, we were all fired up. The rest of the boys removed their shirts in solidarity, which instantly caught the attention of the rest of the women.

The distraction and superior alpha male tennis skills resulted in a predictable 6-0 trouncing. I put my shirt back on and was getting ready to head out with the boys to celebrate when I heard Marci calling out. She jogged up to me and said, "Nick, let's grab a drink. Maybe I can change Twitter's Top Alpha's mind about the ball-girl thing," she said with flirtation oozing out of every pore. I put my arm around her and started walking her back to her group of friends. "Marce, baby, an alpha male always keeps his word. I'll see you tomorrow morning, Court 6, 8am. Sharp." She was disappointed but couldn't hide her smile. I waved the lads over and we all exchanged numbers.

"Thank you, ladies. We're off to Hooters to celebrate with some hot wings and ice-cold domestic beers," I said playfully. "I hope you learned a valuable lesson today."

"We did, Mr. Adams," they said again, nearly in unison.

Perilous territory for alphas

But it's dangerous to be an alpha in professional sports today. Getting blackballed from a league for your beliefs, like Tim Tebow or Enes Kanter Freedom – a dear friend of mine who has supported the work of my organization, the Foundation for Liberty and American Greatness – is one thing. But some alpha males have been on the receiving end of cancel culture, with far more serious consequences.

Look at former Cleveland Indian and Los Angeles Dodgers starting pitcher Trevor Bauer. Bauer first made headlines in 2017 when he revealed on Twitter that he, and most of his Cleveland Indians teammates, were strong supporters of Donald Trump and his America First agenda. As his career blossomed, so did the size of the target on his back. His unabashed support for America and its President, Donald J. Trump, and his unorthodox training regimen. He won his first Cy Young award in 2020 and signed a MASSIVE contract with the Dodgers. Things were looking up for Trevor until it all came crashing down.

In 2021, a San Diego woman with a robust history of chasing after professional athletes accused Bauer of sexual assault. He furiously denied the accusations and provided evidence to back up his claims of a consensual relationship, but in today's world, men are guilty until proven innocent. Despite being cleared by the legal system, he was placed on a seemingly endless "administrative leave" by Major League Baseball for allegedly violating the league's policy on domestic violence and sexual assault

The only problem is that while the sexual acts performed between Bauer and his sexual partner were aggressive, they were, by all accounts, consensual.

Bauer has faced no legal charges and sued the woman who accused him. Despite this, he was essentially suspended for two full seasons. Bauer signed in Japan, where he continued to fight his nasty accuser and sharpen his skills. He won a massive victory in October 2023, when he announced he had settled his litigation against the woman without having to pay her a single cent. He made a brilliant legal maneuver, engaging in his countersuit, not for financial gain but to expose private correspondence from his accuser that she had withheld from law enforcement during the criminal investigation. He took to social media to speak publicly about the details of the situation and reveal damning text messages that proved his innocence.

Below is a transcription of messages between his accuser and her friends, seemingly plotting to fabricate an accusation to extract money from Bauer. She sent a message to a friend before even meeting Bauer that said, "Next victim. Star pitcher for the Dodgers."

"What should I steal?," she set another friend, after her first visit to Bauer's house. "Take his money." her friend replied. "I'm going to his house Wednesday. I already have my hooks in. You know how I roll."

Later on she texted friends, "Net worth is 51 mil. Need daddy to choke me out." "Being an absolute WHORE to try and get in on his 51 million," she sent to another friend. One friend, seemingly the only person in her life with even a hint of conscience, asked her if she felt even a little bit guilty, to which she replied, "not really."

She approached Bauer's legal team multiple times seeking a financial settlement, but each time, Bauer told her resoundingly to GET BENT. He did not waver in maintaining his innocence, he did not cower or apologize. He stood firm, and he won.

Despite his vindication, the proud Trump Republican and Cy Young Winner has had his MLB career destroyed in its prime based on flimsy accusations from a desperate Bat Bunny because "Believe All Women." His reputation was permanently damaged, and he was robbed of tens of millions in earnings.

Chapter 12
Cancel Culture vs. Alpha Males

It's never been more dangerous to be an alpha male. Never mind that alpha males are mostly responsible fathers, loving husbands, successful professionals, and involved citizens. Or that they are the bulwark of Western civilization. The more high-profile the alpha, the more extreme the attacks from the media and cancel culture society.

The examples are endless.

Johnny Depp had his entire career destroyed by false and baseless accusations of sexual assault. It required a full-fledged lawsuit to have his reputation restored.

Drew Brees said he preferred to stand for the anthem, and was intensely attacked from all sides until he eventually walked back his statement.

Andrew Tate was literally banned for being too much of an alpha male and too popular with Generation Z and millennial males. They claimed Tate was causing damage with his 'toxic masculinity.' Tate had 4.7 million followers on Instagram. When TikTok banned Tate, they said: *"Misogyny is a hateful ideology that is not tolerated on TikTok."* The bans followed an online campaign to deplatform Tate, whose influence on his primarily young audience had reportedly, "become a growing concern among parents and teachers."

Phil Mickelson was attacked for joining the LIV Golf Tour with extreme consequences. The previously universally-loved golf superstar was viciously slandered by his peers and the golf media, losing millions in sponsorships as a result. LIV Golf is known for playing tournaments on Trump courses, which no doubt was a driving force behind the coordinated efforts to ostracize Mickelson and his LIV colleagues. Why? Because Mickelson is the top alpha of golf. Dozens of other top-tier golfers made the jump from the PGA Tour to LIV Golf, but the players who received the most intense criticism were masculine American alpha males like Mickelson, Bryson DeChambeau, Brooks Koepka, and Patrick Reed.

And the most obvious case of alpha male censorship anywhere in the world is the writer of this book's foreword and the 45th President of the United States, Donald J. Trump.

The media and Left feel inferior to President Trump. His masculinity and alpha dominance intimidate them so much that they ruthlessly and slanderously attack him on a daily basis. The deep state feels so threatened by his independence and boldness as an outsider they have, at the time of writing, charged him 91 times through four indictments in the span of five months.

Apparently, the greatest criminal of our lifetime is coincidentally the leading opposition to Joe Biden, the current occupant of the White House. Trump leads in virtually every battleground state poll. Liberal prosecutors are engaging in election interference by scrambling to schedule the trials in the middle of the election season to take Trump off the campaign trail.

Then there is the MeToo movement, the perfect example of all alpha males being demonized because of the illegal actions of a few men.

No alpha male supports sexual harassment or assault or rape – in fact, alpha males DETEST men who commit crimes to fulfill their sexual desires with women. Alpha males want to PROTECT women in Western society and ensure they are NEVER in danger of being assaulted or exploited.

Alpha males protect the women they love and are close to. An alpha male would lay his life on the line to protect the woman he loves. A beta male would stand by and do nothing and then play the victim in the aftermath, blaming toxic masculinity and taking no responsibility for his shortcomings as a protector.

No one would ever defend a man who actually commits an illegal sexual act against a woman, but their rights should not be dismissed at the mere accusation from a female. Every legal case in the United States should be treated the same: *innocent until proven guilty*. The MeToo Movement represents and embodies precisely the opposite premise: *guilty until proven innocent.*

"Believe All Women" is one of the worst phrases ever created. I don't believe all women, just like I don't believe all men. People lie regardless of gender. Prince Harry is not inherently more or less honest than Meghan Markle. It's an absurd thing to say. Tragically, it has become the headline phrase for the MeToo movement and has defined how they treat every situation. Just look at what happened to Justice Brett Kavanaugh, a man of extraordinary character who had his livelihood threatened on an accusation that many believe was politically motivated. Where did the accusations come from, and why did they disappear once he was confirmed into the United States Supreme Court

Stand strong. Thrust forward. Never apologize.

If there is one thing I want young men to take away from this book, it's this: Never apologize. Stand up for yourself and your fellow men. There's nothing alpha about letting a woman or a beta male berate you and shame you for being a man or doing what you know is right. FIGHT BACK. Tell them to get bent. One of the biggest lies American women have permeated throughout society is that if someone is berating you, attacking you, or demanding you bend to their wishes, the manly thing to do is sit there and take it on the chin. There is a time for stoicism, but that ain't it.

You are an alpha male. You deserve respect and admiration. You aren't there to "go with the flow," you ARE the flow. Feminists have sought to isolate us. Put us on an island where they dictate the terms of manhood and castrate us to make us more agreeable. Isolation is the first step. Take that golf trip with the boys. Go watch the games at Hooters with the fellows. Get a good pump in at the male-only gym.

You need to learn to stand up for your brothers the way women stand up for each other. Restore the fraternity of alpha males supporting other alpha males. Surround yourself with a support system of masculine guys who will be there to back you up when you're confronted, build you up when you're down, and celebrate with you when you win.

I'll leave you with a story.

As you know, I do a lot of traveling. Being a wildly successful alpha male means I have a packed schedule. I've met a lot of great friends throughout my travels, but sometimes I believe God puts me on certain flights for a reason.

In July of 2023, I arrived at the airport a bit early for flight. I was working diligently on my iPad when something in my peripherals caught my eye. I looked up to see a masked couple take the seats directly across from me. Naturally, my eyes were immediately drawn towards the man. Seeing a ridiculous N95 mask covering his face enraged me. I had to do something. I felt a swell of testosterone as I locked eyes with the man sitting mere feet away from me.

I was seated as I usually am, legs spread wide apart. In doing so, I immediately established that I was the alpha dog in this interaction. He kept his gaze fixed on mine for a moment but quickly began to buckle under the pressure of my stare as he crossed his legs to make room for his effeminate messenger bag.

What was only mere seconds of direct eye contact felt like hours. During that time, I felt like I truly understood the man I was wearing down with my masculinity.

I saw the eyes of a man who had experienced pain. The pain of a man whose masculine aspirations of a foursome with the boys had been crushed by the nasty woman sitting to his left. A man who was bullied out of his fantasy football league by his nagging wife right as his team was on the verge of a dynasty. A man who has allowed his masculinity and agency to be eroded like the Grand Canyon.

My compassion turned to consternation, and I intensified my gaze. This man wasn't a victim. He was a coward. He surrendered his testicles in his quest for female validation and betrayed his own kind.

As soon as I made the slightest lean forward, the other man broke. He averted his gaze from mine, looking directly down and slinking further back into his seat.

"Your mask, son, take it off," I said, leaning forward even further, "it's time you act like a man again." As he reached for his mask, his wife slapped his hand down, "Don't you DARE take that mask off," she said in a shrill tone, "You don't listen to him. You listen to ME."

That was the last straw for me. I stood up and approached the woman as her husband looked up at me like a child watching Superman come to his rescue. I rained hellfire down on this nasty woman, putting her in her place as only a true alpha male could. The entire gate watched in awe as I thoroughly humbled the woman for all to see. When I was finished, the only word she could utter was a shaky "sorry" as she removed her mask.

By this point, her husband had already discarded his mask, and life had returned to his lifeless eyes. He told me his name was Geoffrey, and I offered my outstretched hand with a smile and helped him up. "Come with me. We're going to the concierge to get you upgraded to first class," I said as I put my arm around his shoulder. "You have much to learn."

As luck, or divine providence would have it, our flight was delayed. We left his wife behind and headed to the Admirals Club, where I had booked a private room. I poured two hot black coffees and headed in right behind Geoffrey. Before I closed the door, I affixed a sign that read, "Privacy, please. A new alpha male is being forged today."

A woman lost her subservient husband that day, but the world gained an alpha male. You may remember this story from Twitter, but that's not where it ends. Geoffrey and I became fast friends. He filed for divorce from his wife, who was so humbled by my words that she barely put up a fight. Thankfully for Geoffrey, he had no children, so it was a clean break. We stayed in close communication throughout the process and became close friends. He was a proud Texan, but had relocated to San Francisco after his marriage.

Like so many other men, he had become isolated in the Bay Area. His only source of solace was the occasional 49ers game he could sneak off to when his wife was traveling for work. "Watching Nick Bosa, CMC, and Brock Purdy for 3 hours every week is all I have in this city," he recounted to me once in a text. "But she wouldn't even let me put it on the TV. The only sports she would allow was the occasional Warriors game."

"You're better off without her," I'd constantly remind him. He knew I was right, but divorce is no easy thing. "No pain, no gain." His divorce was finalized about two months prior to this writing. I invited him out to my country club for a weekend of foursomes and red meat. He thrived as he experienced the joys of male friendship for the first time in years. Turns out, he was a great golfer and had an eye for steak. When it came time for the boys and I to send him off, he couldn't bring himself to go back to the land of fruits and nuts. He extended his trip for an extra week and went house hunting. He put in his two weeks notice and listed the condo he had won back from his ex-wife.

Geoffrey is now thriving in the great state of Florida. With the money he saved in taxes, he was able to join an elite country club, where he now regularly hosts foursomes and frequently joins my backyard tackle football games. He's a proud Hooters patron who's taken up with one of the best-looking waitresses in the area. He is living his best life all because one special alpha male had the balls to stand up for his fellow man.

Conclusion

The womanly world will try to bring you down at every turn. I try to recite alpha male affirmations on a regular basis to remind myself that I am an alpha male and nothing can stop me from winning in life. I encourage you to try some of these simple affirmations and watch your life improve:

I am powerful.
I am fearless.
I am prominent.
I am valorous.
I am nimble.
I am lively.
I am perceptive.
I am astute.
I am brawny.
I am gifted.
I am polished.
I am deft.
I am triumphant.
I am versatile.
I am poised.
I am charming.
I am attractive.
I am majestic like a lion.
I am ferocious like a tiger.
I am powerful like a bear.
I am majestic like an eagle.
I am cunning like a fox.
I am passionate like a bull.
I am strong like a horse.
I am at the top of the food chain.
I am an alpha male.

ACKNOWLEDGEMENTS

I have been blessed to have grown up around and been shaped by many alphas in my life.

First and foremost, *my father*.

He taught me everything there is to know about being an alpha. While I can't live up to his standard, I never stop trying every day. He isn't physically with us anymore, but he lives on in my heart, and through my memories.

Second, *President Trump*.

Thank you for agreeing to write this foreword. It is beyond an honor, and I will never forget it. You are the greatest political leader of my lifetime, and the 21st century. You show every day what is possible, and how much one can endure, with an alpha mindset.

To the boys I grew up around and remain ferociously loyal to: *Evan, Sanjay, Garry, Nick, Pete, Mick, Jimmy, Ange, Phil, and Johnny R.*

To the best team that became adopted family, and have helped make my American dream a reality: *Tommy, Texas, and Stackathon – the three greats.*

To the alpha male mentors and father figures: *Greek grandfather, German grandfather, Uncle George, Geoff L, Mr. Amir, Bill J, Sylvester Stallone, Lew H, and Mr. A.*

To quote Willie Nelson, and *"to all the girls I've loved before who now are someone else's wife."*

Cooper, the best and greatest young lady.

My mother, for her constant love and support.